IN-HOUSE TEAM

Editor-in-chief: Caroline Blake

Sub-editor: Mike Toller

Designer: Anja Wohlstrom

Editorial & design assistant: Alexi Duggins

Production consultant: Iain Leslie

Cover design: James Cuddy and Jake Howard

Sales director: Brett MacDougall

National advertising manager: Sue Ostler

Web development: Cameron J Macphail

Accounts and HR: Sharon Evans

Operations director: Martin Dallaghan

Managing director: Ian Merricks

Publisher: IMD Group

Thanks to Katy Georgiou, Laura Jones and all previous contributors and photographers.

LONDON TEAM

City editors: Dan Pilkington, Rebecca Wicks and Emma Howarth.

D1448162

Photography: Visit London, John Ashley, Matthew Bowden, Christopher Bruno, Mirco Delcaldo, Nathalie Dulex, Mark Fletcher, Ibon San Martin Gómez, Antje Ickler, Tim Ireland, Jyn Meyer, Jorge Nassauer, La Rees, Jim Reilly, Laura Sharples, Adrian St Onge, John Tramper and Stephen Cummiskey: National Theatre, William Steward, Ronaldo Taveira, Enver Uçarer, Lina Vili, Tom Stapely, Alex Christie, English Heritage, Sightlines, Lisa Stone, Ben Gilbert, Shauna Scott, Roland Eva, Thilo Weimar, Louise Marlborough, Helen Kennedy, Andreas Jonsson, Peter Spurgeon.

Itchy Media Ltd
White Horse Yard
78 Liverpool Road
London
N1 0QD
Tel: 020 7288 9810
Fax: 020 7288 9815
E-mail: editor@itchymedia.co.uk
Web: www.itchycity.co.uk
ISBN: 1-905705-02-6/978-1-905705-02-3

□□□□□□□□□□□□□□□□□

Welcome to Itchy 2006

We've trawled this green and pleasant land to bring you the finest guide to outing and abouting that our sceptred isle has to offer. We're bruised and battered after the escapades we've carried out in your honour, so the least you can do is follow our trail of destruction. Liver let die, eh? This book is bursting with cool bars, cosy pubs, lazy cafés and budget beds. We'll even tell you where to get hold of a slippery nipple at 4am. Team Itchy all have PhDs in misbehaviour; if it's debauchery you're after, we've got places to pull in and places to pass out in. The culture vultures are catered for too, from Caravaggio through to comedy. We've also done a spot of re-decorating since 2005, so we hope you like the new look. Bright and dynamic; a bit like your good selves. We've even given you shiny symbols to make your life that bit easier (have a gander below). Researched and written by locals, Itchy is your new best mate. So, come on, let's get under the covers...

🕒	Opening hours
🍴	Food
⊘	House wine
💲	Price

Introduction

Welcome to London

Another year, another liver-bashing – put your hands together for London town. Whether you've just rocked up to get your hands on that gold they speak of, or have lived here forever, we're sure you'll find inspiration within our pages. Even if you're a total know-all and have been everywhere before, it'll work as a set of handy reminders. Whatever, you're here now.

So what's new in the city of a thousand tube strikes? Well there's the Ice Bar in Piccadilly (if you like drinking vodka, wearing a parka, hanging out in a fridge). Or you could take a trip to Annexe 3, the new venture from the Lounge Lover boys. It's a temple of veritable indulgence. There's also Dans Le Noir, a new restaurant where you dine in the dark, served by blind waiters. (No jokes about pulling a dog please.) Then there are all the old stalwarts: the parks, the museums, the markets, the freakshows of Leicester Square and Scouser Phil bellowing 'Don't be a sinner, be a winner' at shoppers in Oxford Circus. We're happy to go to hell, just as long as he ain't there.

For us though, this year is about a return to old style boozing - yep, we've finally realised how skint we are. You'll find loads of reviews of proper pubs both old and new, as well as a shedload of restaurants where you can eat for next to nothing. And that doesn't mean they're skanky either. The great thing about London is that once you've accepted you can't eat at Nobu, there are so many cheap and fantastic alternatives you'll forget you ever wanted to. Get thee to Soho for a slap-up meal at Café Emm. Cheap as, errr, chips.

Of course we've reviewed plenty of bars to keep the balance, as well as clubs, shops, cultural stuff and places to crash out in.

This year we've gone for a flash new layout. We're out to dazzle you with style. Londoners are fussy buggers and we're stepping up to the plate to please you.

Tube tips remain as ever, so if you find yourself in zones one or two with some time on your hands we hope we've sorted you out.

OK. That's enough from us for this year. Have a flick, then get out and have it in the UK's coolest city.

* Living in London is like dancing on a shifting carpet, so if you want to let us know that the greasy spoon on your corner has just turned into a burlesque drinking den, drop a line to: editor@itchymedia.co.uk.

Two days in London

SLEEP – If you're up for a night of swanking, the king of cool is Zetter. You'll find it hidden away in Clerkenwell. If that doesn't take your fancy how about the Sanderson? It ain't cheap, but it's well worth it and has high-class toiletries to pilfer.

SHOP – Now you're talking. The markets are a must: try Spitalfields (Sundays) or Portobello (Saturdays). Selfridges is fabulous, darling. Check out the Momo café in the middle of the women's designer section. Other musts are the massive Topshop on Oxford Street and Bond Street for credit card damage.

ATTRACTIONS – The London Eye is a real beauty, as is Tate Modern, Moving away from the river, London's parks are fantastic - try Primrose Hill for celeb spotting or Hyde Park for banter.

EAT – Yauatcha is the hip choice for central London dining. East-enders love Hoxton Apprentice. And the south and west-siders should try Bamboula and Sugar Hut respectively.

DRINK – Try cocktails in Lounge Lover, a sup in CVO Firevault (book a table first), the Phoenix Theatre bar or The French House for a bit of classic pub action.

Two days on the cheap

STAY – St Christopher's Inns are fab for people on a shoestring and if you stay at The Village branch on the Southbank you get a rooftop hot-tub and sauna. Hark at you...

SHOP – No chance. We're allowing you a fiver for tourist tack accidents. Those Big Ben spoons don't half draw you in. You'll be caressing a policeman's helmet before you know it. Ahem.

ATTRACTIONS – You're in the right place. London has a world of freebies on offer (and we don't just mean those freaks that pretend to be statues either). Try the Photographers' Gallery, British Museum or the National Gallery for size. Or just hang out by the river – St Katherine's Dock is great for pretending to be a millionaire.

EAT – Café Emm is a bargain and then some. You'll find similar gems of cheapness at Icco's, Maison Bertaux and Carluccio's. If it's daytime sustenance you're after try the markets – Camden's falafels are fairly legendary and the Hawaiian Pacific stall at Spitalfields market will give you more food than you can shake a stick at for a fiver.

DRINK – You can't go wrong with Nordic - it has a different happy hour every day of the week. Any Sam Smith's pub will serve up cheap ale too. Try the Champion on Wells Street. Our other faves are the Dog & Duck, Lock Tavern, Yorkshire Grey or Gordon's for their commitment to decent prices and a laid-back vibe.

CLUB – Get to Cargo/Herbal before they start charging and stay put 'til closing. Or for the full tilt effect, get down with the beautiful people at the achingly-hip Fabric, our very own super club in Clerkenwell.

wagamama

fast and fresh noodle and rice dishes from london's favourite noodle restaurant

www.wagamama.com

positive eating + positive living

Central

Central

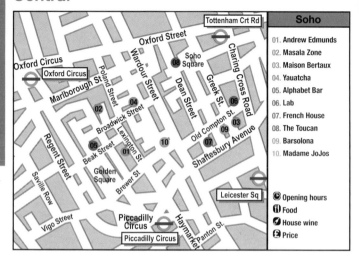

SOHO BARS

Alphabet Bar

61–63 Beak Street, W1
(020) 7439 2190
⊖ Oxford Circus

This place is classic Soho; they serve double measures of spirits automatically and it's always buzzing. It does sometimes fill up with spiritually bankrupt wankers sitting next to each other, talking on their mobiles though. It's rammed at weekends, so get yourself one of the car seats downstairs, before you find yourself crawling round on the map on the floor, trying to find your way home six cocktails later. Go if you think that Nathan Barley is aspirational television.

🕒 *Mon–Fri, 12–11pm; Sat, 4–11pm*
🍷 *Mermaid's pussy, £6.30*

Lab

2 Old Compton Street, W1
(020) 7437 7820
⊖ Tottenham Court Road

The perfect place to experiment with cocktails. We're still working our way through the martinis. Ingredients are top quality and drinks are lovingly prepared. It's all quite high concept – even the ashtrays were specially commissioned – but it's not pretentious, as the 'bitches' and 'pimps' toilet labels and fire-breathing barmen indicate. Trendy Soho-ites still pack the place, and though this is no meat market, you may still want to dress to impress. Ring ahead on busy nights.

🕒 *Mon–Sat, 4pm–12am (late licence sometimes); Sun, 4pm–10.30pm*
💰 *Cocktails start around £5.00 and go up to £17.00 for the Zombie (lethal)*

◻◼◻◻◻◻◻◼◻◻◻◼◻◻◻◻◻

Lucky Voice

52 Poland Street, W1

(020) 7439 3660

⊖ Oxford Circus

Fear not, oh vocally challenged ones. Your strangled cat impression may be less 'Voice of an Angel' than 'Voice of a Mangle' (Mrs), but even you can sing at Lucky Voice. The amount of reverb that the clever bods put in the private rooms at this Tokyo–style Karaoke parlour means that even the most tone-deaf chanteuse will sound alright. Plus, there's a box of wigs and hats that comes with each room, so you'll soon shed your inhibitions. 'But will I be able to avoid singing?' we hear you ask. You should be so lucky; lucky, lucky, lucky.

🕐 *Daily, 6pm–1am*

🅰 *From £20 per hour*

The Player

8 Broadwick Street, W1

(020) 7494 9125

⊖ Tottenham Court Road

You might think you're heading to the wrong kind of Soho night-spot as you squeeze down the dark staircase. Once inside though, you'll find yourself in one of Soho's hippest late-night drinking spots. You may struggle if you can't discuss the new Arctic Monkeys EP, but after a couple of their lethal Moscow mules you'll feel right at home.

🕐 *Mon–Wed, 5.30pm–12am; Thu–Fri, 5.30pm–1am; Sat, 7pm–1am*

🍴 *Chargrilled pork fillet skewers, £5.00*

🍷 *£15*

Two Floors

3 Kingly Street, W1

(020) 7439 1007

⊖ Piccadilly Circus

The only real trendy bar in Soho (so cool they don't have a name above the door), Two Floors's shabby-chic basement is always full of serious-looking creatives. They're too hip to notice newbies, though, so you won't be gawked at. Plus, they all think they're 'it', which can be hilarious, especially in summer when the cool kids sunbathe by the open windows.

🕐 *Mon–Sat, 12am–11pm; Food, 12pm–4pm*

🍴 *Parma ham, mozzarella & basil sandwich, £4*

🍷 *£11*

Central

SOHO PUBS

The Dog and Duck

18 Bateman Street, W1

(020) 7494 0697

⊖ Tottenham Court Road/Leicester Square

Sounds like the start of a filthy limerick. A friend-cull might be necessary before a night out here. Ditch anyone loud, fat or particularly odorous – this pub is fabulous, but absolutely tiny. Assuming you are left with at least one thin, fragrant friend, we reckon you'll dig the Dog & Duck. The whole place is covered top-to-toe in old mosaic tiles, giving it an old-school Victorian vibe. There are ales a'plenty and many excuses for accidentally rubbing people up when you go to the bar, too.

☻ Mon–Fri, 12pm–11pm; Sat, 6pm–11pm; Sun, 7pm–10.30pm

French House

49 Dean Street, W1

(020) 7437 2799

⊖ Leicester Square/Picadilly Circus

Still totally idiosyncratic and more than a little cliquey. When we asked if we could take a photo for this guide there was a full-on debate and vote between the regulars. For the uninitiated there are two key points. 1) Don't order a pint – it's halves only here. 2) Don't ask why it's called French House – everyone who's anyone knows it was the French Resistance centre in WWII. Oddities aside, you should try this place though; it's really rather special.

☻ Mon–Sat, 12pm–11pm; Sun, 12pm–10.30pm; Food Mon–Sat, 12pm–3pm

🍴 Roast pheasant and red cabbage, £11

💰 £13

The Toucan

19 Carlisle Street, W1

(020) 7437 4123

⊖ Tottenham Court Road

Worth an aternoon visit, as it's so rammed at night you'll never get your bearings. A cracking Irish boozer with smiling staff, spot-on Guinness (one of the barmen does different 'beer-foam' pictures), a vast range of whiskeys and talk of the old country. It's easy to go all misty-eyed for the rolling Irish hills amid the relics scattered about the place. A cosy place to plot drunken plans for world domination.

☻ Mon–Fri, 11am–11pm; Sat, 1pm–11pm; Sun, 5.30–10.30pm; Food, Mon–Fri, 11am–3pm

🍴 Mushroom and leek pie, £5.95

💰 £12

SOHO CLUBS

Barsolona

13–17 Old Compton Street, W1

(020) 7734 0623

⊖ Leicester Square

Hidden away right in the heart of Soho, Barsolona is a tiny underground Spanish bar, visible only as a doorway in the middle of the Boheme empire, with Café Boheme and La Boheme on street level. It's well worth investigating as you'll find an excellent range of tapas and jugs of decent sangria for £12.50. Knock a couple of those back and enjoy nightly DJs playing Spanish, Latino, and South American tunes. You could almost be in... errr... Barcelona.

◎ *Mon–Sat, 6pm–3am; Sun, 6pm–10.30pm*

Metro

19–23 Oxford Street, W1

(020) 7437 0964

⊖ Tottenham Court Road

A dark, depressing hole of a venue that happens to host some shit-hot nights. Top of our list is Saturday's Blow Up – the finest mod, 60s and soul night in the land; if you're in town make sure you get down there. Otherwise there's plenty else on offer, including cheap drinks during the week and various indie-rock club nights to keep you going till the weekend. They also do a nice line in up-and-coming bands, so it's a good place to catch the next big thing. Metro isn't pretty, but it knows a good riff when it hears one.

◎ *Gigs from 8pm; Club nights, Tue–Thu 11pm–3am; Fri–Sat, 11pm–4am*

Madame JoJos

8–10 Brewer St, W1

(020) 7734 3040

⊖ Piccadilly Circus

Funky hip-hop nights are the current crowd puller at this classic London venue, but that's by no means all there is on offer. They've been putting on comedy, cabaret and music for decades, but still don't miss a beat. Dress with taking it all off again in mind and prepare for a night of dancing, posing and flirting – in that order. The music comes first here, but there's some talent dotted about the place too. An excellent place for the central London clubber with a low tourist tolerance level.

◎ *Wed–Fri, 10pm–3am; Sat, cabaret 7pm–10pm; Sat, club, 10pm–3am; Sun, 9pm–3am*

Central

SOHO CAFÉS

Beetroot

92 Berwick Street, W1

(020) 7437 8591

🚇 Leicester Square

One you find this small but delicious-smelling café in the depths of Soho, you'll never lose your way again. The smiling staff look so cute in their aprons, some almost as tasty as the buffet of organic and vegan delights that sits aside the orange 'kiddy' tables. Try the lasagne, shepherd's pie and their famous coleslaw with lemon and dill. And don't you dare leave without taking some carrot cake with you. This is where you make up for all those lousy kebab nights. Divine.

© *Mon–Sat, 9am–9.15; Sun, closed.*

Maison Bertaux

28 Greek Street, W1

(0871) 332 1672

🚇 Leicester Square

The problem with pressing your face against the window to see better is that the glass tends to mist up and obscure the very wet-dream-inducing vision of glistening pastry, pink chiffon, and fairy lights you were trying to drool over in the first place. Better to squeeze inside this pocket of faded Parisian charm and immerse yourself in the ragged memorabilia and rickety furniture. You may need to re-mortgage your second home in Chelsea to afford a cake, but it really is worth it. Sacre-bleu, these rosbifs don't know they're born.

© *Mon–Sat, 8am–11pm; Sun, 8am–8pm*

🍴 *Quiche, £3.30*

SOHO RESTAURANTS

Andrew Edmunds

46 Lexington Street, W1

(020) 7437 5708

🚇 Oxford Circus

Cramped? Cosy? Couldn't care less, as this restaurant is just so romantic. Take a sexy diva for a divine evening. Be warned though, that the décor is basic, only the food here is modern. Upstairs, it looks like a shabby French restaurant but downstairs is a candlelit emerald cove… so downstairs every time. The food is fantastic, the service charming and the prices reasonable.

© *Mon–Sat, 6–10.45pm; Sun, 6–10.30pm*

🍴 *Braised rabbit with cream, tarragon and white wine, £11.25*

💷 *£11.50*

Café Emm

17 Frith Street, W1
(0207) 7437 0723
⊖ Piccadilly Circus

If you're on some poncey diet, you'll hate it here. This is a restaurant of the old school; concessions to carb-free are few and far between. Music to our ears. And as for the prices, Cafe Emm's cheap and cheerful menu will win you serious brownie points with whoever's paying. It's not romantic or somewhere to impress with, but for boozy work-dos, dates with your best mate and couples past the flirting stage, it's perfect.

ℂ *Mon–Fri, 12pm-2.30pm & 5.30pm–10.30pm; Sat, 1pm–4pm & 5pm–11.30pm; Sun, 1pm–10.30pm*

ℳ *Poached haddock fillet, £8.95*

∅ *£9.90*

Yauatcha

15 Broadwick Street, W1
(020) 7494 8888
⊖ Tottenham Court Road

Yauatcha has a bit of reputation as a 'place to see and be seen', but that's never put anyone off. We're perfectly happy with the slick décor, tasty dim sum and oriental-style French patisserie goods. We reckon you will be too, if you manage to get a booking (its current status is 'always rammed'). A fuss has been made about Yauatcha's decision to have 90-minute sittings in the restaurant – we can't say it made any difference to our night here.

ℂ *Mon–Fri, 12pm–11pm; Sat, 11am–11pm; Sun, 11am–10pm*

ℳ *Braised sweet and sour pork, £7.80*

∅ *£19*

Masala Zone

9 Marshall Street, W1
(020) 7287 9966
⊖ Piccadilly Circus

Curry-by-numbers, classy chain style. Are you with us or shall we elaborate? Ok then. Masala Zone dishes up well-prepared Indian food in a canteen-style setting. Punters are trendy-ish types who didn't get round to going when it first opened and wayward tourists looking jolly pleased with themselves. And so they should: ignore the plastic-wrapped chainy feel and you've struck gold with this restaurant.

ℂ *Mon–Fri, 12pm–3pm & 5pm–11pm; Sat, 12pm–11.30pm; Sun, 12.30pm–3.30pm & 6.30pm–10.30pm*

ℳ *Butter chicken, £6.55*

∅ *£10*

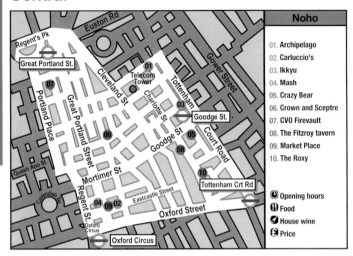

Noho

01. Archipelago
02. Carluccio's
03. Ikkyu
04. Mash
05. Crazy Bear
06. Crown and Sceptre
07. CVO Firevault
08. The Fitzroy tavern
09. Market Place
10. The Roxy

🕐 Opening hours
🍴 Food
🍷 House wine
💷 Price

NOHO BARS

Bradley's Spanish Bar

42–44 Hanway Street, W1

(020) 7636 0359

⊖ Tottenham Court Road

Every time we're here we become embroiled in some sort of burgeoning office romance. It seems to be that kind of place, with drunken girls fumbling over their bosses, married men 'accidentally' snogging the girl from accounts and general chaos ensuing by closing. Sometimes there are x-rated gropings in the corner, others it's tears before bedtime and puking on the streets. It's far more civilised than this review might suggest, with the best jukebox in London.

🕐 *Mon–Sat, 11am–11pm; Sun, 12pm–10pm*

💷 *£11.80*

Crazy Bear

26–28 Whitfield Street, W1

(020) 7631 0088

⊖ Goodge Street/Warren Street

If it wasn't for the gun to our heads, we wouldn't even be writing this. But it seems there's no bargaining with the Itchy mafia. Not where spot-on party venues are concerned... and this place (gritted teeth, twisted arm, alright then, for Christ's sake you animals) is hot. From the discreet and very low-key entrance (marked by a bear scratch) to the seemingly random locale, this bar has got it going on. It's one big, fabulous, London love-in; the perfect place for partying, and celebrations.

🕐 *Mon–Fri, 12pm–11pm; Sat, 6pm–11pm*

🍴 *Charolais beef fillet, £11*

💷 *£11*

Hakkasan

8 Hanway Place, W1

(020) 7907 1888

⊖ Tottenham Court Road

Michelin-starred Hakkasan is a fine place for a celebration as long as you mean serious business – it's as expensive as it is stylish. If dim sum and modern Chinese mains don't take your fancy (or sound like financial suicide), head for the adjoining bar and mingle your way through the fabulously unusual cocktail menu. It's all a bit JLo, so dress to impress and be prepared to spend a small fortune on a round.

☻ *Mon–Wed, 12pm–3pm & 6pm–11.30pm; Thu–Sun, 12pm–3pm & 6pm–12.30am*

⑪ *King scallops in yakiniku sauce, £22*

❷ *£24*

Loom

5 Clipstone Street, W1

(020) 7436 0035

⊖ Great Portland Street

Tucked away somewhere off Great Portland Street lies one of the capital's undiscovered treats. During the week the venue's intimately lit alcoves make it a great place to go for a ca tch–up with friends, but come Friday night this cosy, basement bar is packed full of sloaney studenty types lamenting the difficulty of life with only daddy's cheque–book to fall back on. The first or last Friday of each month sees a night from pop aficionados 'Team We Love You', with a joyous selection of tunes.

☻ *Mon–Fri, 12pm–1am; Sat, 7pm–1am*

⑪ *Brie and redcurrant tart, £5.70*

❷ *£10.50*

Nordic

25 Newman Street, W1

(020) 7631 3174

⊖ Goodge Street/Tottenham Court Road

If you've been reading this section waiting for us to come up with somewhere that doesn't require a remortgage/robbery/date with a rich but fat man, here's your answer. Roll up, poor people, there's a fine happy hour to be had at Nordic. There's also the enticing possibility of hot Swedish minxes/menfolk on either side of the bar (though we realised on our visit they're not all lithe, blonde and up for it). Food is smorgasbord-tastic and drinks cover all bases with a lot of emphasis on vodka. Skol!

☻ *Mon–Fri, 12pm–11pm; Sat, 6pm–11pm; Sun, closed*

⑪ *Swedish meatballs, £7.85*

❷ *£9.75*

Central

NOHO PUBS

Crown & Sceptre

86 Great Titchfield Street, W1

(020) 7307 9971

⊖ Great Portland Street

Nicely situated amongst the international eateries just off Great Portland St., this pub has become a haven for BBC masses and waiting-to-be-seen media sluts. On the right day, its eclectic furnishings, high windows and encompassing horseshoe bar can be a genuine treat. On others, the overloud music and shouting clientele are enough to make you stick a bread knife in the toaster. Nice line in beers, though, if you can catch the bar staffs' eye.

◉ *Mon–Sat, 12pm–11pm; Sun, 12pm–10.30pm; Food, Mon–Sun, 12pm–9.30pm*

The Fitzroy Tavern

16 Charlotte Street, W1

(020) 7580 3714

⊖ Goodge Street/Tottenham Court Road

Once the drinking hole of 1930s writers, poets and bohemians, The Fitzroy is an important London pub. It's all very cosy, old school and bizarrely inspiring. You'll leave thinking you're the modern incarnation of Dylan Thomas, swinging round lamp posts and bemoaning your misunderstood genius. All well and good until you wake up in the morning, remember you're an electrician and that your girlfriend dumped you on the number 25 home. Still, we're sure it was worth it.

◉ *Mon–Sat, 11am–11pm; Sun, 12–10.30pm; Food, Sat–Thu 12–2.30pm & 7pm–9.30pm; Fri, 12–2.30pm*

The Newman Arms

23 Rathbone Street, W1

(020) 7636 1127

⊖ Goodge Street/ Tottenham Court Road

Pie-muncher centralis, with an entire upstairs room devoted to all things meaty and pastry-encased. You only have to sink your teeth into one to see why. We're not talking your standard flaccid pub effort, these pies are so good they've even won an award for them. They've had a bit of a refurb this year, and although we miss the tartan and horse brass look upstairs, we have to admit that it's brightened things up considerably. The only thing we can't guarantee is a place to rest your arse for the evening; this place, despite its loveliness is tiny.

◉ *Mon–Fri, 12pm–11pm; Food, Mon–Thu, 12pm–3pm & 6pm–8.30pm; Fri, 12pm–3pm*

NOHO CLUBS

Market Place

11 Market Place, W1

(020) 7079 2020

⊖ Oxford Circus

An excellent, if sometimes painfully loud place to spend an evening, we're still in love with Market Place. The top floor houses the hectic drinkers on a mission, while downstairs is more chilled. You won't be able to shake the feeling that you've accidentally stepped into a sauna, but go with it and tuck into decent snacky food and unusual beers. The crowd is young, funky and always up for it.

🕔 *Mon–Wed, 12pm–12am; Thu–Sat, 12pm–1am; Sun, 12pm–10.30pm*

🍴 *Lamb and coriander meatballs, £4.50*

💰 *£12*

The Roxy

3–5 Rathbone Place, W1

(020) 7255 1098

⊖ Tottenham Court Road

Formerly after work suit haven fleapit The Office, The Roxy had a mild makeover (we're talking Richard and Judy, not Trinny and Susannah), and remerged as a West End party venue par excellence. OK, so it's not cool in any shape or form although Tuesday's Panic pulls a well-dressed indie student crowd. No, we're more interested in the messy Thursday night guitar tune heaven that's fuelled by two Kronenburgs for three quid. So if you've had a hard week, get acquainted with the friendly doormen and ask the spiky-haired DJ if he's got any Menswear.

🕔 *Mon-Thu, 5pm-3am; Fri, 5pm-3.30am; Sat, 9.30pm-3.30am*

The Social

5 Little Portland St, W1

(020) 7636 4992

⊖ Oxford Circus

The nursery food concept has really started to grate – but all credit to the Social, they were the first to come up with the idea of charging upwards of £3 for the kind of food your mum used to make when she was in one of her moods. The Social still has it going on, even years down the line. The DJs remain cutting edge, the vibe is funky and the decor looks as good as it did when they opened. Upstairs is best for chilling with your mates, whereas downstairs fits the bill for pissed-up booty-shaking and chat-up missions.

🕔 *Mon-Sat, 12pm-12am*

🍴 *Pie with mash, £6.20*

💰 *£11.50*

Central

NOHO RESTAURANTS

Archipelago
110 Whitfield Street, W1
(020) 7383 3346
⊖ Warren Street

Those who favour familiarity on their plates should stay away from this place at all costs. Yet if you're looking for excitement and adventure, go ahead and take your taste buds on the culinary journey of a lifetime. Sitting in an Aladdin's cave of artefacts as eclectic as the menu, you can challenge your eating preconceptions with wacky weirdness like peacock fritters and crocodile steak.

◉ *Mon–Fri, 12pm–3pm & 6pm–11pm; Sat, 6pm–11pm; Sun, closed*
⑪ *Set lunch, £15.50*
❷ *£16.50*

Carluccio's Caffé
8 Market Place, W1
(020) 7636 2228
⊖ Oxford Circus

Still top of our list for alfresco eating in central London, Carluccio's looks like it'd cost and arm, a leg and a couple of internal organs, but provided you order wisely, it actually verges on cheap. Inside it's bright, white and airy, outside has heaters for cooler nights and plenty of space in the sun when it's hot. Menu-wise, go for salads, breads, olives, pasta (not the ravioli – it's too small) or risotto. Great for dates, catch-ups and shopping lunches.

◉ *Mon–Fri, 7.30am–11pm; Sat, 10am–11pm; Sun, 11am–10pm*
⑪ *Spaghetti vongole, £6.50*
❷ *£10.50*

CVO Firevault
36 Great Titchfield Street, W1
(020) 7580 5333
⊖ Oxford Circus

If you're meeting up with someone you shouldn't, we reckon you should do it here. It's the last place anyone would think to look and the furtive, mysterious air makes even the dodgiest dealings seem glamorous. There are swanky cocktails, champagnes and bar snacks; there's a small outdoor garden; there are beers and wines for the so-inclined and a fabulously exclusive feel. The food is quite expensive, but you get what you pay for, and once in a while, everyone needs a treat.

◉ *Mon–Fri, 12pm–10pm; Sat, 12pm–6pm; Food, Mon–Fri, 9.30am–9pm; Sat, 10am–5pm*
⑪ *Pan-fried salmon, £15*
❷ *£14*

Icco Pizza

46 Goodge Street, W1
(020) 7580 9688
⊖ **Goodge Street**

This place still beggars belief in London town. Pizza for £3? With gastro pubs left, right and centre charging twelfty pounds for wood-fired gnats, it's a relief to see a spot of honest pricing. And just as you start tutting about nasty frozen pizzas, these guys are rolling out the dough before your very eyes and throw the toppings on liberally too. The place itself is always buzzing, with a European cafe society feel in the morning, revving up for an MTV crowd in the evening. Get yourself a pizza the action.

🕲 *Mon–Fri, 7am–11pm; Sat–Sun,*
9am–1pm

Ikkyu

67 Tottenham Court Road, W1
(020) 7636 9280
⊖ **Goodge Street**

Fantastic, bustling basement restaurant serving authentic Japanese dishes to London natives and tourists alike. You'll love the concoction of small temptations served up as the waitresses flail around the tables, with the mackerel set standing up to rigorous Japanese inspection. Be brave and try the sea urchins. Unpretentious but classy nonetheless, it's perfect for an after-work bite to eat, not so great for that hot date.

🕲 *Mon–Fri, 12–2.30pm; Mon–Fri & Sun,*
6–10.30pm; Sat, closed
🍴 *From £1.50 per piece of sushi*
❷ *£11*

Mash

19–21 Great Portland Street, W1
(020) 7637 5555
⊖ **Oxford Circus**

Eating at Mash isn't exactly cheap, but you won't be disappointed if you sit down to dinner here; the chef clearly knows what he's doing. Sci-fi fans will feel at home. The restaurant looks like a cross between a space station and a laboratory, due mainly to the fact that the huge vats at the far end are actually a micro-brewery. Music is provided by DJs in the bar downstairs, which, if you like it loud, is the perfect place to get mashed with an after-dinner cocktail or three.

🕲 *Mon–Fri, 10pm–3pm & 6pm–11pm;*
Sat, 6pm–11pm
🍴 *12oz Welsh côte de boeuf, £16.50*
❷ *£13*

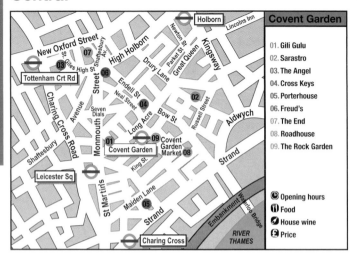

Covent Garden

01. Gili Gulu
02. Sarastro
03. The Angel
04. Cross Keys
05. Porterhouse
06. Freud's
07. The End
08. Roadhouse
09. The Rock Garden

🕐 Opening hours
🍴 Food
🍷 House wine
💰 Price

RIVER THAMES

COVENT GARDEN BARS

Bunker

41 Earlham Street, WC2

(020) 7240 0606

⊖ Covent Garden

Where once stood the Freedom Brewing Co – after hours playground for boozehound business types – now lies Bunker. The microbrewery remains with bizarre copper tubing snaking around behind glass screens. There are still plenty of interesting beers to work your way through, booze-soaking bar food and high spirits. There are also cocktails for the ladies, weekend DJs and the odd showing of the footy.

🕐 *Mon–Sat, 12pm–11pm; Sun, 12pm–10pm*

💰 *£13.50*

Freud's

198 Shaftesbury Avenue, WC2

(020) 7240 9933

⊖ Tottenham Court Road/Covent Garden

Resembling a stage set of a back alley, with a cast who sit at slate tables or on granite steps beside the bomb-shelter toilets, the basement café bar gallery of Freuds is as unique and all encompassing as its clientele. Daytime coffee drinkers give way to lunching shoppers who depart when the out-for-the-nighters arrive. There's calming jazz on Sundays. Itchy warning: steep steps + concrete floor + cocktails = potential ER experience.

🕐 *Mon–Sat, 11am–11pm;*
Sun, 12pm–10.30pm

🍴 *Sandwiches, £5*

💰 *Cocktails, £4–£6*

COVENT GARDEN PUBS

The Angel

61 St Giles High Street, WC2
(020) 7240 2876
⊖ Tottenham Court Road

The Angel is seemingly untouched by the London commercial bar scene. It's surprisingly pleasant, snug and busy inside, attracting the local performing artsy Covent Garden bunch, keen for a few Sam Smith ales. Between Tottenham Court Road and Covent Garden, The Angel is a perfect pint pit stop. Meet your mates here for a few quickly served bevvys before you hit your overpriced West End bars. You'll be pleased you did.

Ⓒ *Mon–Fri, 11.30am–11pm; Sat, 12pm–11pm; Sun, 12pm–10.30pm*

The Cove

1 The Piazza, WC2
(020) 7836 8336
⊖ Covent Garden

If you can find it (head for the Cornish Pasty Co. and up the secret staircase), you might find yourself pleasantly surprised by this Cornish theme pub that seems a million miles from the usual soulless drinking holes of Covent Garden. Authentic Cornish ales mix agreeably with authentic and delicious pasties from the shop downstairs, the perfect accompaniment to a few pints of Betty Stooges or Knocker. Get a seat on the balcony and watch the world go by or laugh at people crammed into the Punch & Judy next door. Pasties… the new Kebab. Fact.

Ⓒ *Mon–Wed, 12pm–12am; Thu, 12pm–1am Fri–Sat, 12–2am*

Cross Keys

31 Endell Street, WC2
(020) 7836 5185
⊖ Covent Garden

A fine old-fashioned boozer, which despite being a stone's throw from Covent Garden's rip-off joints, manages a cosy, fuss-free feel. The pub is in a grade II listed building, though you'd barely know it for the jungle of leaves covering the walls, and the inside is similarly cluttered with everything from copper kettles to Beatles memorabilia. Somewhere to pop your head round the door, check for space (it gets busy at times) and relax with a pint. No pink cocktails, fancy glassware or girls called Harriet allowed.

Ⓒ *Mon–Sat, 11am–11pm; Sun, 12pm–10.30pm; Food, Mon–Sun, 12pm–2.30pm*

Central

Lamb & Flag

33 Rose Street, WC2

(020) 7497 9504

⊖ Covent Garden/Leicester Square

A lovely, but busy, pub full of office slaves and knackered looking folk that remember Peter Andre and Noel Edmonds the first time round. Join their jaded ranks for good old-fashioned spints of ale, dry-roasted peanuts and a glass of dry white wine for the lady. This really is one of Covent Garden's best boozers, it's just you'll never get to see it through the heaving throng. Why not try abseiling or paragliding down onto the cobbled alleyway instead?

☺ *Mon–Sat, 11am–11pm; Sun, 12pm–10.30pm; Food, Mon–Sun, 12pm–3pm; sandwiches 'til 4pm*

Porterhouse

21–2 Maiden Lane, WC2

(020) 7836 9931

⊖ Covent Garden

Take a compass, crampons and some clean underwear – not only will you need superior orienteering skills to find your way round the place, there's also a good chance you'll pull. With this many drunk people under one roof there's got to be someone who likes your particular brand of dishevelled incompetence. It's an Irish pub and the Guinness is as good as you'd find in Dublin, or so a very drunk, teary-eyed gentleman told us.

☺ *Mon–Sat, 11am–11pm; Sun, 12pm–10.30pm; Food, Mon–Sun, 12pm–9pm*

🍔 *Burger, £7.95*

❷ *£11.95*

Punch & Judy

40 The Market, WC2

(020) 7379 0923

⊖ Covent Garden

Last time we were in here a man puked in his shoe and then attempted to drink it. This was voted 'hilarious' by his ten loud Kiwi mates and means we now offer wide berths to anyone with an accent that puts a 'sex' in 'six'. We're sure the Punch and Judy will enable you to develop your own random hatred, so we won't elaborate too much. If you can bear to step inside its sweaty, meat-market pit of skank that is. Seriously, we like you and advise you not to bother.

☺ *Mon–Sat, 11am–11pm; Sun, 12pm–10.30pm; Food, Mon–Sat, 11am–7pm; Sun, 12pm–6pm*

□ ■ □ □ □ □ □ □ □ □ □ □ □ □ □ □

COVENT GARDEN CLUBS

The End

18 West Central Street, WC1

(020) 7419 9199

⊖ Tottenham Court Road

In the beginning (well, ten years ago) a couple of DJ mates decided to launch a venue that showcased the best underground music in the plushest of clubbing environments. They succeeded. Their vision has evolved into a clubbing-world Mecca where all your needs are pampered and stroked into an after-hours frenzy. To the joy of the clubbing fraternity, it always turns out alright in The End.

☻ *Mon, 10.30pm–3am; Wed, 11.30pm–3am; Thu, 10pm–4am; Fri, 10.30pm–6.30am; Sat, 10pm–7am; Sun, 10pm–7am*

The Rock Garden

6/7 The Piazza, WC2

(020) 7836 4052

⊖ Covent Garden

Throughout its time, the Rock Garden has seen an assortment of unsigned bands come through its doors, such as Iron Maiden and The Smiths. The tradition continues every Sunday with a live 'battle of the bands' night. An eclectic range of grooves every other night of the week will cater for every taste and despite the banging crowd, it still retains its smoky, cavern feel to this day. The Gardening Club restaurant provides an excellent meal, as well as an assortment of light bites downstairs.

☻ *Sun–Thu, 11am to 12am; Fri–Sat, 11am–1am*

Roadhouse

The Piazza, WC2

(020) 7240 6001

⊖ Covent Garden

Frankly, this is one to dodge; unless you're prancing around town in an anorak and a rucksack, looking lost. Look to your left or your right and there are countless bars in your midst. Why anyone would actually choose to go here for a night out, we're not quite sure. If you do decide to go, perhaps you could conduct some sort of survey on our behalf, because we sure as hell ain't stepping inside this slag-pit of mediocre bands and chart house ever again. Cheers.

☻ *Bands, Mon, 7.30pm; Tue–Fri, 7pm; Sat, 9pm; Club from 11pm*

Central

COVENT GARDEN CAFES

Kastner and Ovens

52 Floral Street. WC2

(020) 7836 2700

⊖ Covent Garden

The ultimate sandwich shop that seems to serve the whole of Covent Garden, be it ballet dancers, office workers or policeman. Everything is freshly made in the kitchens downstairs and these are definitely sandwiches with attitude, be it feta and caramelised peppers or a very mature cheddar and green tomato chutney. If you're not impressed at the range of pies, pasties and a selection of soups, you will be hooked by the seductive shelves of cakes and pastries.

☺ Mon–Fri, 8am–5pm

COVENT GARDEN RESTAURANTS

Assa

53 St Giles High Street, WC2

(020) 7240 8256

⊖ Tottenham Court Road

'Emergency, which service please?' 'Fire brigade!' 'Please state your location and the exact nature of the emergency?' 'I'm in a Korean restaurant and my mouth is on fire.' 'I'm sorry sir?' 'Send help, please!' 'How do you mean, sir?' 'Well, I ordered this pork and noodle stew and it's all so bloody spicy my mouth is on fire.' 'Have you tried drinking some water sir?' 'I have, but that hasn't helped.' 'Time for bed, sir'.

☺ Mon–Sat, 12pm–12am; Sun, 4pm–12am

🍴 Pork and kimchi stew, £9

Bertorelli's

44a Floral Street. WC2

(0871) 075 1685

⊖ Covent Garden

Bertorelli's has a calm, quiet atmosphere, keeping in tune with the fact that the Opera House is right opposite. The regulars are usually people who want to discuss the show over a glass of wine, although it does have customers who come just for their favourites. The manager, Paolo, a nice man from Italy who knows his food, can help you pick out what you want to eat, or drink. If you smoke, be prepared to be sent to your corner for being a bad boy and spend the rest of your evening with your rib cage pressing into the table for lack of space.

☺ Mon–Sun, 12pm–3pm & 5.30pm–11.30pm

Gili Gulu

50–52 Monmouth Street, WC2

(020) 7379 6888

⊖ Covent Garden

Yet another conveyor-belt sushi restaurant for the good folk of central London. Gili Gulu is certainly not the best example in town though it is possibly the cheapest. A set meal is £7.50 – choose five plates off the belt and a bowl of miso. We were half-expecting a Japanese karaoke singer to appear from the central spiral staircase and choose one lucky punter to vault over their tempura and climb to the heavens. That would have spiced things up more than the wasabi.

🕒 *Mon–Thu, 3pm–5.30pm & 6pm–11pm; Fri–Sun, 12pm–11.30pm*

🍴 *Set meals, £7.50*

💲 *£9.50*

Sarastro

126 Drury Lane, WC2

(020) 7836 0101

⊖ Covent Garden

Dine in this gloriously kitsch operatic extravaganza in the heart of Theatreland and you'll be chatting about the décor all evening. Your eyes take time to adjust to the gaudy, verging on tacky opera–house theme. It has faux–gilded balconies; murals of reclining nudes and a bizarre assortment of theatrical bric–a–brac, but amicable staff and live opera on Sundays and Mondays make for a surreal yet enjoyable experience. But all in all, Sarastro offers more of a visual feast than a culinary one.

🕒 *Mon–Sun, 12pm–12am*

🍴 *Big boss seafood selection, £14.50*

💲 *£13.50*

Hamburger Union

4–6 Garrick Street, WC2

(020) 7379 0412

⊖ Covent Garden

Take a break from whatever kind of hell this world of consumerism is putting you through and join the queue at this homage to our old friend the burger. There'll be none of your flaccid innards and manky fries malarkey here. No, no. no. Here you're looking at a prime beef, chicken, steak, chorizo or veggie (try the halloumi – it's great) burger, grilled to order and served up with all the trimmings in record time. Almost healthy.

🕒 *Sun–Mon, 11.30am–9.30pm; Tue–Sat, 11.30am–10.30pm*

🍴 *Union burger, £3.95*

💲 *£10.95*

Central

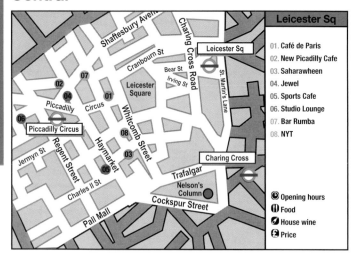

Leicester Sq

01. Café de Paris
02. New Picadilly Cafe
03. Saharawheen
04. Jewel
05. Sports Cafe
06. Studio Lounge
07. Bar Rumba
08. NYT

🕐 Opening hours
🍴 Food
🍷 House wine
💷 Price

LEICESTER SQUARE BARS

Le Beaujolais

25 Litchfield Street, WC2

(0871) 223 6797

⊖ Leicester Square

Francophiles beware. Just off Charing Cross Road this place really sucks you in. In contrast to the tourist traps of the surrounding area, Le Beaujolais is a small, cosy, popular wine bar with French staff and an all ages clientele. The blues music and old 'Ricard' posters just add to the vibe. Relax with a bottle of red and be seduced. Even better, take someone you want to seduce.

🕐 *Mon–Fri, 12pm–11pm; Sat, 5pm–11pm; Sun, 12pm–10.30pm*

🍴 *French fare for around £10.00*

💷 *£12.70*

Cork & Bottle

44–46 Cranbourn Street, WC2

(020) 7734 7807

⊖ Leicester Square

A dad's bar, but mum's invited. She'll be pleased to see that nothing's changed here since the 70s. That's not to say there's no fun to be had here, because really, there is, and it's pretty handily located, so there's no reason not to pop in. It makes a change from the other hell-holes in tourist centrale. The wine list is huge, so order away and make sure you give the food a go too, because there's nothing quite like it.

🕐 *Mon–Sat, 11am–11.30pm; Sun, 12pm–10.30pm*

🍴 *Spicy California sausages with chips, 8.95*

💷 *£12.50*

Ice Bar

31–33 Heddon Street, W1

(020) 287 9192

⊖ Piccadilly Circus

Absolut aficionados will be pleased to hear that the people at Icebar have found the perfect way to keep your drink chilled to the very last drop: they've built a bar made entirely from blocks of ice, imported from Sweden. The walls are ice, the bar is ice, the seats are ice, the décor is ice, even the glasses are little hollow blocks of ice. You get a reindeer cape and mittens to keep the chill out. Take the £15 entrance fee, buy a whole bottle of vodka, put on a parka and climb in your own fridge instead.

🕐 *Mon–Wed, 12.30pm–11pm; Thu–Fri, 12.30pm–11.45pm; Sun, 12.30pm–10.15pm*

💲 *£15 for one drink (includes entrance)*

Jewel

4–6 Glasshouse Street, W1

(020) 7439 4990

⊖ Piccadilly Circus

The walls of Jewel are lined with tiny mirrors for the vain clientele to admire themselves. What's the theme? Is it Arabesque? Is it French? We're not entirely sure. The seating is Spanish Inquisition steel back-breakers. The rest of the decor comes from a land called Fancy Dan. Jewel will not suit anyone who drinks pints, that's the dividing line. Get suited and booted, get a classy dame or fella on your arm and saunter in and out admiring yourself with the other fancy-panted cocktail drinkers.

🕐 *Daily, 5pm–1am*

💲 *Melon martini, £5*

Salvador & Amanda

8 Great Newport Street, WC2

(020) 7240 1551

⊖ Leicester Square

When this place was The Saint we thought it was crap. Now it's got a poncey new name, a refurb, a vaguely interesting looking menu and... is still crap. We didn't really expect much else, so we weren't disappointed. However, it seems busy enough, so it obviously does the job for the kind of people that choose to meet their friends round this bit of town. People who don't care about service, atmosphere, being ripped off, crap food or music that sounds like it should be in a car ad.

🕐 *Mon–Thu, 5pm–3am; Fri–Sat, 4pm–3am*

🍴 *Tapas dishes, around £5*

💲 *£12*

Central

Sports Cafe

80 Haymarket, SW1
(020) 7839 8300
⊖ Piccadilly Circus

Deserves a mention every year because if you're in London for the weekend and there's a match you have to see, this is one of the only central places that shows non-London teams in action. There are screens galore, beers a'plenty and the kind of food you can eat without taking your eyes off the screen, which is just as well, because it looks like the cook was probably also watching the game while it was cooking.

Ⓒ *Mon–Thu, 12pm–2am; Fri–Sat, 12pm–3am; Sun, 12pm–12am*
Ⓘ *8oz 'knockout' fillet steak, £14.95*
Ⓩ *£9.95*

Studio Lounge

5th Floor, Waterstone's, 203–206 Piccadilly, W1
(020) 7851 2433
⊖ Piccadilly Circus

A unique bar that fills the void for somewhere calm and civilised around the Piccadilly region. Pop up here for classy, snacky food, an excellent view of the London skyline (across Trafalgar Square and Westminster) and a cheeky glass of red. It's never gonna be rock'n'roll, it'll always feel like a bookshop (you can read your new selections here), but you'll be so darned glad you found the place.

Ⓒ *Mon–Sat, 11am–11pm; Sun, 12pm–6pm; Food, Mon–Sat, 12pm–4pm & 6pm–9pm; Sun, 12pm–5pm*
Ⓘ *Beef and mushroom pie £8.50*
Ⓩ *£13.50*

LEICESTER SQUARE PUBS

De Hems

11 Macclesfield Street, W1
(020) 7437 2494
⊖ Leicester Square

A Dutch pub this may well be but please don't rock up off your head on your mate Baz's homemade base and demand to know where the bongs are. It's not that kind of Dutch. What it is, is a cosy, atmospheric little boozer in which to kick back with an Oranjeboom and breathe in the scent of days gone by. There are lots of attractive Amsterdam hip-kids in here. Offer them a drink, then demand they split the cost with you. Ah, the old gags really are the best.

Ⓒ *Mon–Sat, 12pm–12am; Sun, 12pm–10.30pm*

LEICESTER SQUARE CLUBS

Bar Rumba

36 Shaftesbury Avenue, WC1
(020) 7287 6933
⊖ Piccadilly Circus

Still a decent destination for a midweek night out – we know, we can't quite believe it's still hanging in there either – with nights spanning the garage/Latino gap and a lot in between. Come the weekend it gets completely packed out with thrill-seeking tourists. During the week, though it suits us fine for late night boozing and a bit of a half-hearted boogie. Funnily enough, the only music they don't play is rumba, which is just as well, because we've tried it and we just looked silly.

Ⓔ *Mon–Thu, 9pm–3.30am; Fri, 10pm–4am; Sat, 9pm–4am; Sun, 9pm–2am*

Café de Paris

4 Coventry Street, W1
(020) 7734 7700
⊖ Leicester Square

If the frighteningly tactile strangers and and not quite up to date dance music aren't enough to put you off returning here, the drinks prices – which necessitate a second mortgage – really should. Don't be fooled by the chandeliers and plush sofas. This is your traditional old-man-in-suit-touches-young-girl-in-skirt kind of establishment, except with a sneaky, expensive veneer slapped on. One to avoid – unless of course you've already consumed a metric shedload of alcohol and don't know any better. Sweaty, tacky and overrated.

Ⓔ *Mon, Tue & Sun, 7–11pm; Wed, 6pm–9:30pm; Thu–Sat, 10pm–4am*

NYT

Whitcomb Court, Whitcomb Street, WC2
(020) 7581 1158
⊖ Leicester Square

This is officially the coolest club Leicester Square has ever had. Kate Moss has graced it with her presence and they'll even let you in wearing trainers – as long as you're incredibly stylish, beautiful and hip and famous, that is. There's going to be a period in which admittance will be as per door-bitch whim but give it a few months and they'll be much more accommodating. Until then, try calling ahead to guarantee entrance. Just be sure to rock up with a Mariah-stylee entourage of 632 bouncers to keep up appearances.

Ⓔ *Wed–Fri, 10pm–3am; Sat, 10pm–4am*

Central

LEICESTER SQUARE CAFÉS

New Piccadilly Café

8 Denman Street, W1

(020) 7437 8530

⊖ Piccadilly Circus

The original and utterly the best; for over 50 years, The New Picc has been serving its classic caff fare to the good, not-so good and plain bad of Soho and Piccadilly. Pimps, popstars, punks and princes have all sat at the formica tables and tucked into plates of ham, egg and chips, fish and chips, or apple pie with lashings of custard. The best thing about this place is that it still looks exactly the same as when the Mods came and smashed the windows.

🄲 *Mon–Sun, 12pm-8.30pm*

🄵 *Lasagne with pesto, £4.50*

LEICESTER SQUARE RESTAURANTS

Café Koha

11 St. Martin's Court, WC2

(020) 7497 0282

⊖ Leicester Square

Around the corner from the midriff–bearing, heaving masses of Leicester Square nestles St. Martin's Court – a parallel universe with surprisingly charming eateries. Café Koha is one of those. It's run by Kosovan brothers who pride themselves on catering for regulars as well as the pre–theatre posse. Koha's olive green walls and a light sprinkling of tack are a welcome relief after tourist centrale.

🄲 *Mon–Sun, 10am–5pm & 5pm–11pm*

🄵 *Koha staff spicy burger, £8.50*

🄿 *£14*

Saharaween

3 Panton Street

(020) 7930 2777

⊖ Piccadilly Circus

This tiny Turkish delight is tucked away behind the totally chav Tiger Tiger, so head on past the cheese-fest and feast on real charm. Saharaween is the kind of place you see and wish you knew about ages ago. Downstairs is an Aladdin's cave of cushions and couples making eyes over candlelit portions of moderately priced Eastern cuisine. Tasty, tender stews, moorish (ahem) cous cous and best of all, a BYO policy make this one to remember next time you have a date to impress.

🄲 *Daily, 4pm–1am*

🄵 *Chicken tagine, £9.50*

🄿 *BYO*

'ALLO ME OLD CHINA

CHINATOWN: EVERY COSMOPOLITAN CITY WORTH ITS SALT NEEDS ONE. AND BOY, HAS LONDON GOT ONE.

From Chuen Cheng Ku's fleet of clattering trolleys serving dim sum the bona fide Hong Kong way, to the institution of comically rude service that is **Wong Kei**, the Gerrard Street area shovels on the authenticity as thick as the MSG. For the less squeamish amongst you, once you've made it past the gallery of skinned ducks hanging in the window, **Canton** serves up some of the most genuine old-school cuisine in the area; just don't expect any attention to décor. The votes are out as to where in Chinatown does the best food (at least in part due to the size of the cleavers many of the chefs own), but many regulars claim that **Mr Kong** regularly hits the spot. However, for those of you who are willing to venture a little further , **Yming** definitely does the best grub 500 metres away from the main drag.

Canton – 11 Newport Place, WC2 . 020 7437 6220
Chuen Cheng Ku – 7 Wardour Street, W1. 020 7437 1398
Mr Kong – 21 Lisle Street, WC2. 020 7437 7341/9679
Wong Kei – 43–46 Wardour Street, W1. 020 7437 8408
Yming – 35–36 Greek Street, WC1. 020 7734 2721

Central

BLOOMSBURY

Bloomsbury Bowling
Basement of the Tavistock Hotel, Bedford Way, WC1
(020) 7691 2610
⊖ Russell Square/Goodge Street

Scene of an Itchy showdown earlier this year, these bowling lanes are a godsend. And if bowling doesn't float your boat, they've got private karaoke rooms, a mini-cinema and 60s-style girl bands singing on a Saturday nights. If you're still curling your lip, they've got an Americana diner for you to gorge at. They even have wi-fi to lure the students to their lair. Perfect place for a birthday party or perhaps to bowl a maiden over?

◐ *Mon-Tue, 11am-1am; Wed, 11am-2am; Thu-Sat, 11am-3am; Sun,11am-12am*
◑ *£5.50 per game*

Planet Organic
22 Torrington Place, WC1
(020) 7436 1929
⊖ Goodge Street

This deli-come-mini-supermarket is a health-lover's heaven. You'll find everything from the expected, like organic fruit, to the unexpected and slightly bizarre, like organic make up. Gillian McKeith would have a bloody field day. If you're feeling all wholesome (and also happen to be something other than skint) then try some deli treats, and if you're feeling really generous buy yourself a smoothie. Keep reminding yourself it's organic and maybe then paying £3 for liquidised fruit won't seem so bad.

◐ *Mon-Fri, 8am-9pm; Sat, 10am-7.30pm*

Tas
22 Bloomsbury Street, WC1
(020) 7637 4555
⊖ Goodge Street

Tas very much wears its heart on its sleeve. A bright and bustling Turkish restaurant near the British Museum, the food is very reasonable with a menu almost baffling in its unfettered choice. The set menus are excellent and while its proximity to tourism havens means it's a favourite for families, it remains an excellent addition to the hit Anatolian mini-chain for a bite of an evening. They've got loads of long tables, so it's perfect for a birthday dinner.

◐ *Mon-Sat, 12pm-11.30 pm; Sun, 12pm-10.30 pm*
Ⓘ *Kofte, £7.95*
◉ *£11.95*

CHARING CROSS

Gordon's Wine Bar

47 Villiers Street, WC2

(020) 7930 1408

⊖ Embankment/Charing Cross

Somewhere, under London's busy streets, an ancient wine cellar lies hidden from the chaos of the city above. There, people meet to sit at low tables under soot-blackened arches. They meet to add their voices to the echoes of 200 years of animated conversation. They meet, as those before them did, to drink wines of unsurpassed quality and eat fine cheeses from around the world. Your life will be bettter for having fallen back up the stairs at Gordon's.

☾ *Mon–Sat, 11am-11pm; Sun, 12am-10pm*

✪ *£11.70*

Ship and Shovell

1–3 Craven Passage, WC2

(020) 7839 1311

⊖ Charing Cross

When is a pub not a pub? Well, when it's two pubs. Let us explain: the Ship and Shovell is dissected by a little passage, meaning the pub is split into two completely separate bits. Each side comes complete with its own bar, door, sign, barstaff, rambling drunkard propping up the bar etc, but it's still one pub. Strange, but it works. Regulars will swear that one bit is better than the other, but they're just trying to justify why they spend so much time there. Itchy likes both, equally. If you're meeting someone there, just be sure to tell them which half you'll be in.

☾ *Mon–Sat, 11am-11.30pm; Sun, closed;*
Food, Mon–Sat, 11am-3pm

Queen Mary Boat

Waterloo Pier, Victoria Embankment, WC2

(020) 7240 9404

⊖ Embankment

The Thames may have been declared biologically dead a few decades ago, but the Queen Mary's made damn sure that it's not socially dead. An ideal venue for summer drinking, the top deck of this boat, permanently moored off the Victoria Embankment, showcases the Thames in all its beauty. A word of warning though: try not to lose your coordination up here, as any beer bottles you knock off the side won't end up in the river, but will most likely clock someone on the deck below. You never know, you might even get lucky and spot the next whale.

☾ *Mon–Thu, 12pm–11pm; Fri–Sat,*
12pm–2am; Sun, 12pm-10.30pm

Central

HOLBORN

Na Zdrowie

11 Little Turnstile, WC1

(020) 7831 9679

⊖ Holborn

For a crazed night of vodka excess, this is the place to be. Tucked away behind Holborn tube, it's miles from the nearest tourist and well worth a look. The vodka list is huge and there's Polish inspired bar food for the so inclined. Punters are an array of clever types feeling smug at their find and drunken students taking a break from the revolution.

☺ *Mon–Fri, 12.30pm–11pm; Sat, 6pm–11pm; Food, Mon–Fri, 12.30pm–10pm; Sat, 6pm–11pm*

Ⓘ *Polish sausage and mash, £6.50*

☻ *£10*

The Perseverance

63 Lamb's Conduit Street, WC1

(020) 7405 8278

⊖ Holborn

When mid-1990's retro comes back into fashion, this place will be the dogs. Until then you'll just have to make do with a perfectly pleasant boozer. Like the fat kid at school who wants to be cool but isn't, this place does all the right things but fails to inspire. But the food is good (especially Sunday lunch) and if the clamour of enthusiastic self-starters gets too much, there's another room upstairs, complete with calming candles.

☺ *Mon–Sat, 12–11pm; Sun, 12–10.30pm; Food, Mon–Sat, 12pm–3pm & 6.30pm–10.30pm; Sun, 12pm–4pm*

Ⓘ *Venison sausages, £10.50*

☻ *£12.70*

Ye Olde Cheshire Cheese

145 Fleet Street, EC4

(020) 7353 6170

⊖ Blackfriars

Entering through the side alley entrance, expecting to bump into Hagrid or at very least a small goblin trying to sell you a dragon's egg or two, thankfully your polite and perfectly dressed waiter will lead you into what initially seems to be London's very own Leaky Cauldron. With its mahogany rooms and original 17th-century features (seriously), you can't fail to fall under the cheesy spell.

☺ *Mon–Sat, 11.30am–11pm; Sun, 12pm–3pm; Restaurant, Mon–Fri, 12pm–9.30pm; Sat, 12pm–2.30 & 6pm–9.30pm; Sun, 12pm–2.30pm*

Ⓘ *Vegetable Wellington, £8.95*

MARYLEBONE

Lowlife

34a Paddington Street, W1

(020) 7935 1272

⊖ Baker Street

Some say dingy, we prefer underground.
Lowlife looks like it could be too cool
for school, but they're having none of it.
Pretension doesn't get a look in. There's no
room. In fact even the live music acts have
to wedge themselves in. Friendly staff serve
cocktails and, if it's privacy you're after,
you can sneak into an intimate hideaway.
Lounge on the comfy retro furniture.

🕙 *Mon–Fri, 12pm–11pm; Sat, 6pm–11pm;
Sun 4pm–10.30pm & 12pm–2.30pm; Food,
12pm–9.30pm*

🍴 *£10.50*

Prince Regent

71 Marylebone High Street, W1

(020) 7467 3811

⊖ Baker Street

A haven for metrosexuals, this smoky
pub draws the younger crowd with loud
music and live singers on Wednesdays.
If you don't have to wait half an hour
to be served, you'll enjoy the decently
priced bevvies and it's a really good
joint to pick up a potential pull. In
the summer, they wheel out some
bizarre fluffy parasols and things spill
out onto the high street. Keep your
eyes peeled for Madonna (she lives
round the corner). Then mingle over
a few pints and take your pick of
the marvellous Marylebone masses.

🕙 *Mon–Sat, 12–11pm; Sun, 12–10.30pm*

The Providores

109 Marylebone High Street, W1

(020) 7935 6175

⊖ Bond Street/Baker Street

If you find yourself in the West End with
a hangover and 25 quid in your pocket,
try brunch at the Tapa Room It's buzzing
and very loud but the staff are pleasant and
service is reasonably quick. Warning! This is
no greasy spoon, anyone with a man-sized
appetite would need two platefuls (but
would probably resent paying for them). It's
overpriced but if you didn't impress him/her
last night, you will do here the morning after.

🕙 *Mon–Fri, 9am–11.30am & 12pm–10.30pm;
Sat, 10am–3pm & 4pm–10 30pm; Sun,
10pm–3pm & 4pm–10pm*

🍴 *Bacon fry-up, £8.60*

🍴 *Freshly squeezed orange juice, £4*

Central

EDGWARE ROAD

Al - Dar

61–63 Edgware Road, W2
(020) 7402 2541
⊖ Marble Arch

This traditional Lebanese restaurant is great if you're looking for authentic Middle-Eastern food. It's also pretty good if you're looking for a rich husband. The place doesn't stand out from other Lebanese restaurants, but the food is fabulous and cheap. And if chillis get you hot and bothered this is perfect as Arab food is known to be mild. For the complete experience make sure you try sheesha. Just don't sheesh and drive, eh?.

🕒 Mon–Sun, 8am–1am
🍴 Lamb shawarma, £3.25

Maroush

21 Edgware Road, W2
(020) 723 0773
⊖ Marble Arch

There are a few of these in London but not all of them have all-singing, all-dancing belly dancers for you at the weekend, who gyrate around your tables, swinging wobbly bits about that may well make or break your otherwise tasty hummus experience. The stuffed lamb is excellent. In fact, we've never heard any complaints about this Middle-Eastern treat, except perhaps that the staff can be a little slow. But so would you be if you spent the whole night ogling wiggling belly dancers.

🕒 Daily, 12pm–2am
🍴 Main courses, £14–22

Windsor Castle

27–29 Crawford Place, W1
(020) 7723 4371
⊖ Edgware Road

The glass-encased sentry guard outside the door should give you some clue of the eccentricities you're about to find inside. This pub is home to the Handlebar Club, a group of dapper gents with a penchant for waxing their facial hair. If you want to see old buffers, in all their hirsute glory, they meet on the first Friday of every month. Brush up your bumfluff to see if you can pass their muster. As if that wasn't enough, they also have a gallery of stars on the wall (including a signed pic of Pele) and a cracking Thai kitchen.

🕒 Mon-Sat, 11am-11pm;
Sun, 12pm-10.30pm

HIGH-RISE BARS

TOP BARS WITH CRACKING VIEWS

Windows on the World

Hilton, 22 Park Lane, W1

020 7208 4021

Hyde Park

Make like every wealthy male heir in LA and get yourself inside a Hilton. As with all these venues, it's a highly classy affair, so make sure you dress smart, and are prepared to shell out. But in terms of the view, you get what you pay for, and the stunning vista from the 28th floor will have even the biggest skinflint smiling.

Tate Modern Rooftop

Bankside, SE1

020 7887 8888

Blackfriars/Southwark

After you've finished getting your fill of culture, the bar at the Tate Modern offers a stylish restaurant with a great view, complete with bar. The perfect place to go settle down with your friends, stroke your chins and discuss the meaning of modern art. Members get to sit out on the roof, so try to pull a culture vulture on your way round.

Vertigo

25 Old Board Street, EC2

020 7877 784

Bank

No Hitchcock references, just superb views of London, on the 24th floor of the City's tallest building, Tower 42. It may be pricey, but what else do you expect from drinking in a bar that finds you higher than the London Eye? Be warned: it's quite small so you may want to try and get there as early as possible to avoid

The Heights

Langham Place, W1

020 7580 0111

Oxford Circus

After a serious stint of retail therapy, nip up Regent's Street to St George's hotel. Hurtle up to the tenth floor to find the 'wall of windows' and, more importantly, the bar. It's not particularly flash, but they do half-price cocktails during happy hour (5–7pm, oddly enough). This place is also a celeb-stalkers paradise, with the BBC headquarters next door.

CALLING ALL ASPIRING JOURNALISTS AND PHOTOGRAPHERS...

We need daring writers and hawk-eye snappers to contribute their sparkling talents to the launch issue of Itchy magazine.

We want the inside track on the bars, pubs, clubs and restaurants in your city, as well as longer features and dynamic pictures to represent the comedy, art, music, theatre, cinema and sport scenes in your city.

If you're interested in getting involved, please send examples of your writing or photography to: editor@itchymedia.co.uk, clearly stating which city you can work in. All work will be fully credited.

Bath/Birmingham/Brighton/Bristol/Cardiff/Edinburgh/Glasgow/
Leeds/Liverpool/London/Manchester/Nottingham/
Oxford/Sheffield/York

North

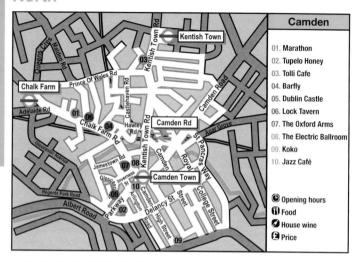

Camden

01. Marathon
02. Tupelo Honey
03. Tolli Cafe
04. Barfly
05. Dublin Castle
06. Lock Tavern
07. The Oxford Arms
08. The Electric Ballroom
09. Koko
10. Jazz Café

🕐 Opening hours
🍴 Food
🍷 House wine
💲 Price

CAMDEN BARS

Barfly

49 Chalk Farm Road, NW1
(020) 7916 1049
🚇 Chalk Farm/Camden Town

Now giving their name to the place (it used to be known as the Monarch) as well as putting on great gigs, the Barfly crew have cleaned up in Camden. This is still one of the best places in town for catching bands on the up (and sometimes down). See them first, hone your stalking technique and prepare for plenty of 'way back when' tales to tell your grandchildren. Don your rock'n'roll attire and join the revolution.

🕐 *Mon–Sun, 7pm–12am, but varies according to gigs*

Bar Vinyl

6 Inverness Street, NW1
(020) 7681 7898
🚇 Camden Town

We love Camden for its gothic gatherers, whiffs of pot, dodgy pizza and up until recently, stall after stall of mind-altering mushrooms. But there are also those who loathe the place for it. Luckily, Bar Vinyl seems to break down the barriers and invites everyone in for a party. This narrow, cosy bar, with its red pleather seating, live DJs and ever-changing local artwork always seems to buzz. Go early and join the chatter with a coffee, or late to jump around like an idiot with the people who've been there all day.

🕐 *Mon–Sat, 11am–11pm;*
Sun, 12pm–10.30pm

CAMDEN PUBS

Caernarvon Castle

7 Chalk Farm Road, NW1

(020) 7284 0219

⊖ Camden Town

Renowned for showcasing hot new talent…
or just the musical wannabees needing
to add Camden to their list of gig venues,
there's never a shortage of music to jump
around to if you head here in the evenings.
They specialise in axe-fiends (calm down,
we're only talking guitars here) playing
Guns'n'Roses covers, but it's always
rammed. Given the location, it's surprisingly
lacking in goth-gatherings. Perhaps they're
all still sitting on the bridge drinking cider?

Ⓒ *Mon–Sat, 12pm–11pm;*

Sun, 12pm–10.30pm

Crown and Goose

100 Arlington Road, NW1

(020) 7485 8008

⊖ Camden Town

Tucked just off Camden High Street,
this the foodie's drinking den. Its good
looks (dark green walls and mismatched
chairs, with the odd antique thrown
in) and beautiful crowd (mostly media
types judging by the number of mullet/
mohican do's) make this cosy space
instantly likeable. As well as being pretty
to look at it's also just pretty cheap. A
real gem of a pub – what's good for
the Goose is well worth a gander….

Ⓒ *Mon–Sat, 12am–11pm; Sun, 12pm–10.30pm*

Dublin Castle

Parkway, NW1

(020) 7485 1773

⊖ Camden Town

Looking like it took interior design tips
from the local working men's club
(fly posters, shoddy-looking furniture
and a couple of old boys thrown in for
authenticity), this low-key pub has a
large back room where you can watch
bands (from Madness to newbies) play
for about £5 entry. A well-manned bar
with friendly staff means that getting
served involves very little hassle. A
scruffy pub with musical character.

Ⓒ *Mon–Sat, 11am–12am ; Sun, 11am–10.30pm*

**Due to last year's re-jigging of licensing hours, you can get a drink up to the
closing times listed, but you might get some bonus drinking time too. Result!** *Itchy*

Lock Tavern

35 Chalk Farm Road, NW1

(020) 7482 7163

⊖ Chalk Farm/Camden Town

Still packing 'em in like they're giving it away, the cult of the Lock is showing no signs of a backlash. And no wonder when they offer MTV stars, muso types and bar staff that look like they have modelling contracts. Not to mention the beer garden, roof terrace, pies, cocktails, beers and spot-on fabulous DJs. Ok, so the mood isn't quite as buzzy as it was in the early days, but a place like this can do without the bleedin' edge posse for a few weeks.

◐ *Mon–Sat, 12pm–11pm; Sun, 12pm–10.30pm; Food, Mon–Sat, 12pm–5pm & 6.30pm–9pm; Sun, 12pm–5.30pm & 7.30pm–9.30pm*

The Old Eagle

251 Royal College Street, NW1

(0871) 984 2618

⊖ Camden Town/Mornington Crescent

The Old Eagle is an unpretentious, rustically decorated pub with attentive and friendly staff. Think green tiles and ivy. It's popular with the locals, but without the traditional, unwelcoming locals' 'greeting' of a silent stare. This drinking den's worth bearing in mind if you're looking for somewhere slightly off the beaten track, where you can find a rickety seat or beaten-up sofa and fritter away a happy afternoon with a gang of pals. Please keep it to yourselves. We all need a quiet jar and a sit down now and again.

◐ *Mon–Sat, 12pm–11pm; Sun, 12pm–10.30pm*

The Oxford Arms

265 Camden High Street, NW1

(020) 7267 4945

⊖ Camden Town

If it's a pint, football and a sturdy meal you're after then this is a safe bet. Once you've torn yourself away from the gathering of Goth's outside and actually found the door, you can settle in (or out the back) for a while. The Sunday roast is £6 – a bit tight on roast potatoes, but with mash as well you can't complain. Slightly shabby inside, but relaxed with pierced locals and market-goers. Plenty of booze, plasma screens, plus Etcetera theatre upstairs make it a more than acceptable Camden hide-out.

◐ *Mon–Thu,11am–12am; Fri–Sat, 11am–1am; Food until 9pm*

CAMDEN CLUBS

The Electric Ballroom

184 Camden High Street, NW1

(020) 7284 0745

⊖ Camden Town

A favourite for Goths, disco kids, students and any one else who regularly frequents Camden Lock on a Saturday afternoon, the Electric Ballroom is a shabby glorious mess, but one that has quite a history of services to alternative music, be it indie guitar bands or full-on techno - although Saturday nights are a straightforward chart mess. A great venue for seeing big names playing preview/fanclub only gigs, just make sure you've applied your eyeliner before you get in the queue for Fridays.

🎵 *Fri-Sat, 7.30pm-3am*

Koko

1a Camden High Street, NW1

(0870) 432 5527

⊖ Mornington Crescent

The former Camden Palace is a melodramatic and cavernous space which houses a variety of club nights and gigs from R'n'B to gigs from the likes of Madonna. Most noticeably, it is the home of Camden's current hot ticket for trendy youngsters, Friday's 'Club NME'. At this night, you will feel old if you're not wearing footless tights (girls), hats (boys) or lashings of eyeliner (both). Can get cold and the drinks aren't cheap but the space is suited to a good night out, if only because it's so big you can avoid that disastrous snog from earlier.

🎵 *Times vary, according to gigs*

Jazz Café

5 Parkway, NW1

(020) 7916 6060

⊖ Camden Town

Founded in 1990, the Jazz Café has trodden a path of booking artists that other big venues can't or won't risk booking, as well as hosting some seriously jumping club nights. Far from being exclusively jazz, funk, soul and hip-hop are staples of the Jazz Café, and the young and hip crowd make it a million miles away from the studied, smoky ambience of Ronnie Scott's amongst others. The fizzing atmosphere is compensation for an often over-crowded venue that ain't exactly cheap. Put on your shiny dancing shoes.

🎵 *Mon-Sun, 7pm-2am*

CAMDEN CAFÉS

Tolli Café/Restaurant

Kentish Town Road, NW5

(020) 7267 0911

🚇 Kentish Town

Pop in to Tolli for the best latte you can imagine. Serving delicious pasta, sandwiches and other such Italian foodstuffs, Tolli is the perfect place to quieten that roaring lunchtime stomach grumble. Just watch out for the pirates decorating the walls – they may just give you a knowing wink. That's got you thinking. The waitresses don't speak the best English, so please be kind.

🕐 Mon–Fri, 8am–7pm; Sat, 8am–6pm; Sun, closed

🍴 Pasta with spinach, £5.20

CAMDEN RESTAURANTS

Haché

24 Inverness Street, NW1

(020) 7485 9100

🚇 Camden Town

In a quaint little restaurant on a bubbly side-street in Camden, a revolution has started to sizzle and spit. To those that thought a place called Haché in Camden Town might sell something other than Grade A food, we recommend they go and get themselves probably the best burger they've ever tasted; with a big heap of chips, of course.

🕐 Mon–Sat, 12pm–10.30pm; Sun, 12pm–10pm

🍴 Steak le grand, £9.95

💰 £9.95

L'écluse

3 Chalk Farm Road, NW1

(020) 7267 1012

🚇 Camden Town

Being very close to the lock, this relatively small restaurant can have people waiting patiently for a table, but they're mainly tourists who probably haven't seen anything else in the area to capture their imagination – aside from bongs and mohawks. The food is ok, but instantly forgettable. You'd probably have a nicer experience in the market with some cheap Chinese from a stall. At least there you get the odd smile from a passing stranger, which you sure as hell won't get from the staff in here. Don't bother.

🕐 Mon–Sat, 12pm–11pm; Sun, 12pm–10.30pm

Mango Rooms

10–12 Kentish Town Road, NW1

(020) 7482 5865

⊖ Camden Town

The food in this place is about as Caribbean as a bag of dried coconut shavings. What we mean is you have to put the effort in behind the 'packaging' to get a decent result. As a venue it's quite fun and colourful – the tables are large so great for groups and if you're out for a good time and a few cocktails this would be perfect. However, for authentic West Indian dishes it doesn't deliver. Most are verging on bland, which is a shame as it's a great location for bar–hopping afterwards..

🕒 *Mon–Sun, 12–11pm*

🍴 *Creole snapper fillet, £10*

💲 *£11.95*

Tupelo Honey

27 Parkway, NW1

(0871) 332 5709

⊖ Camden Town

Like bees to the honey pot flock the dudes to this local gem – a calm and tasteful 'cool-free' shop. The token attractive staff have the odd pepper grinder shoved up their waste disposal units, which kind of detracts from the decency of the Modern European food. Don't be alarmed though, if you're good looking, you'll be welcomed with a luke warm chiselled smile. There's a great fireplace, perfect for a wintery night with a glass of rouge and a good flirt with someone as cool as you.

🕒 *Mon–Wed, 10am–9pm; Fri–Sat,*
10am–11pm; Sun, 10am–8pm

🍴 *Honey mustard chicken sandwich, £4*

Marathon

87 Chalk Farm Road, NW1

(020) 7485 3814

⊖ Camden Town

There are some combinations that shouldn't work, but do. Strawberries and black pepper; peas and ketchup; Richard and Judy. Totally illogical, but strangely good. Marathon have taken this concept one step further. At the front is a room that looks like a normal kebab shop. In fact, it is a kebab shop. At the back, though, is a jazz club. Admittedly, they only do the jazz thing on Friday and Saturday nights, but then they do it properly. Absolutely bleedin' mental. Noel Gallagher pops in every now and again.

🕒 *Sun-Thu, 11am-2am; Fri-Sat, 11am-4am*

🍴 *Large doner kebab, £4*

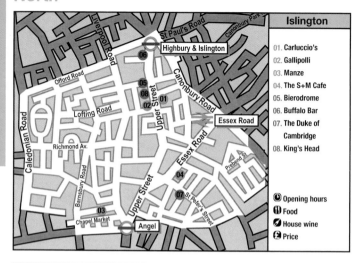

Islington

01. Carluccio's
02. Gallipolli
03. Manze
04. The S+M Cafe
05. Bierodrome
06. Buffalo Bar
07. The Duke of Cambridge
08. King's Head

⊙ Opening hours
🍴 Food
🍷 House wine
💷 Price

ISLINGTON BARS

Bierodrome

173–174 Upper Street, N1
(020) 7226 5835
⊖ Highbury & Islington/Angel

Belgian theme-bar anyone? Didn't think so... but give Bierodrome a go and you might just be pleasantly surprised. From rich dark chocolate beers, to one that tasted of strawberries. You can be sure of an alcohol content that would knock most Stella drinkers sideways and a hangover that will see you through till the next working week. If you don't fancy taking on the Belgian's with an empty stomach, then accompany your beer with a bowl of French fries.

⊙ *Sun–Thu, 12pm–12am;*
Fri & Sat, 12pm–2am

BRB @ The Arc

1 Torrens Street, N1
(020) 7837 9421
⊖ Angel

This funky bar starts buzzing around seven-ish and the rest, as they say, is history. Like its clientele, BRB is sophisticated, hip and happening. Even better are their Tuesdays when you can get a '2 for 1' offer on their pizzas. The ambience means that the place is great for big birthday parties or tête-à-tête intimacy in an alcove. We liks that kinda range. Our only word of caution would be to go easy on the drinks or you'll have reached your (Visa) limit quicker than your flexible friends.

⊙ *Mon–Sat, 11am–11pm;*
Sun, 11am–10.30pm

Buffalo Bar

295 Upper Street, N1

(020) 7359 6191

⊖ Angel

A tiny place tucked away under Highbury and Islington tube, it's the perfect place to impress with your knowledge of the underground music scene (literally underground in this case), and a great venue to see the Donkey Ballbreakers before they hit the big time. The sound is fantastic, you'll pretty much be on stage with the band, and its candle-lit ambience is really rather charming for a music venue. The regular Artrocker nights will even have you dancing to some old indie hits. All this and not a stuffed buffalo in sight.

© Mon–Sat, 8.30pm–1am

ISLINGTON PUBS

The Angelic

57 Liverpool Road, N1

(020) 7278 8433

⊖ Angel

One of those pubs that manages to be all things to all people most of the time. Whether it's the yummy mummys tucking into the juice bar during the day or the old men and office types fighting for bar space by night. Unlike most of Itchy's favourite haunts it's light and airy, almost romantic, and the food's top notch. A wishing well and piped Shakespeare make for an interestingly cultural trip to the lav.

© Mon–Sat, 12pm-11pm;
Sun, 12pm-10.30pm

🍴 Lamb hot pot, £10

Embassy

119 Essex Road, N1

(020) 7226 9849

⊖ Angel

An old classic nowadays but still a fine place to slink into a corner, get down to some cracking tunes and rejoice that they still haven't put the bar prices up. Embassy is still refreshing, despite the hundreds of clones you'll find all over town. They did the working men's club style décor before everyone else started copying and their punters are loyal. Loyal and damned attractive, if you want our opinion, which let's face it, is all you're going to get here, take a wad of fivers and your little black book. You won't leave disappointed.

© Mon–Thu, 5pm–11.30pm; Fri–Sat,
5pm–1am; Sun, 5pm–10.30pm

The Duke of Cambridge

30 St Peter's Street, N1

(020) 7359 3066

⊖ Angel

The Duke of Cambridge is a thoughtful old chap. He serves only organic food and drink, to ensure minimal environmental impact and a minimal hangover, so don't be shy with the organic wines and lagers. The food is not for the faint hearted and the menu – changing twice daily, neglects no part of organically reared animals – serving up everything from hide to head. The Duke packs a regular Islington crowd within its exposed brick bar and candlelit restaurant, especially on Sundays, when they come in their droves for the award-winning organic roasts.

Ⓒ *Mon-Sat, 12pm–11pm; Sun, 12pm–10.30pm*

Filthy McNasty's

68 Amwell Street, EC1

(020) 7837 6067

⊖ Angel

Irish muso boozer that packs 'em in night after night. Pitch up and knock back a Guinness or two with the starry, rock'n'roll clientele. We've spotted the odd Libertine in here on more than one occasion and there's always some serious action going down. Drinking is hardcore – they're the only place we've found north of the Thames with Red Stripe on tap – and partying is an art form for the stylish crowd at Filthy's.

Ⓒ *Mon-Sat, 12pm–11pm; Sun, 12pm–10.30pm; Food, Mon-Sun, 12pm–3pm*

Ⓜ *Thai green curry, £5*

Ⓐ *£12.50*

King's Head

115 Upper Street, N1

(020) 7226 0364

⊖ Angel

The best late drinks in Islington. The King's Head Theatre Bar opens late every night offering drinks, live music and a wanker-free zone to N1's mad, bad and dispossessed. There'll be a man with hair to his ankles singing about the old days and ten girls from Finland clinking vodkas in time to the music. You'll walk in, feel like a regular and leave drunk and happy when they chuck you out. Just how we like it.

Ⓒ *Mon-Thu, 11am–12am; Fri-Sat, 11am–1am; Sun, 12pm–12am*

Ⓜ *Pre-theatre, three-course set meal, £14*

Ⓐ *£13*

ISLINGTON CLUBS

Carling Academy

16 Parkfield Street, N1

(020) 7288 4400

⊖ Angel

We had our reservations when the chaps at Carling decided to install one of their rock'n'roll machines deep in the bowels of a shopping centre, but so far, so good. Although the live acts that come to N1 aren't as big as those at the sister venues, they're just as good, with recent shows by the likes of Graham Coxon and Frankie Goes To Hollywood. The Academy really comes into its own with its clubnights, ranging from efforts by the likes of XFM to nights such as Feeling Gloomy.

◉ *Times vary according to gigs*

The Garage

22 Highbury Corner, N5

(020) 7607 1818

⊖ Highbury & Islington

If you loved the experience, the sights, sounds and smells of darkened, slippery, lager stained floors associated with indie nights of the 1990s, come to the Garage. It promises to be one of the best venues for every indie kid out there. On Fridays, Alan McGee and Danny Watson showcase the latest live new talent and on Saturdays the 'International Hi-Fi 'night will keep those out of date Oasis haircuts bobbing. Live out your punk fantasies alongside foot-long Mohican clad rockers every other Saturday with Steve Lamacq's 'Punk Rock Karaoke'. Classic alternative weekender.

◉ *Fri–Sat, 11pm–3am*

Electrowerkz

7 Torrens Street, N1

(020) 7837 6419

⊖ Angel

Electrowerkz is still bringing us the ultimate night to end all club nights, '100% Dynamite', to the masses. Head to this laid-back warehouse venue for the best reggae night in London town, with Trojan Record's DJs playing chilled-out rocksteady and ska. Best dig out yer braces and piano ties then. The rest of the time they play host to an ever-changing array of experimental club nights for folks who like to be there at the very beginning of the next big thing. We've already got our coats on. We'll see you in the queue.

◉ *Fri–Sat, 9pm–late*

ISLINGTON CAFÉS

Alpino

97 Chapel Market, N1

(020) 7837 8330

⊖ Angel

From the outside, it mightn't look like much, but inside, Alpino is a little wonderland of fading varnish wooden booths, red–leather seating, colourful local characters, and all the kitsch charm you'd expect of a caff that's been sorting 'em out since 1959. . If you're after a slice of authentic London cafe culture, as well as the kind of entertaining service that could have come straight out of the Albert Square caff, then get yerself dahn to Alpino. And say hello to Team Itchy wolfing their lunch.

☻ *Mon–Sun, 6.30am–4pm*

Manze

74 Chapel Market, N1

(020) 7837 5270

⊖ Angel

You can't get a lot more quintessentially cockney than a pie and mash shop and Manze's on Chapel Market in Islington is one of the best at least. Its traditional tiles and wooden stalls evoke memories of Ealing comedies and Bow bells but the food is excellent and fantastically cheap. A small pie and mash will set you back no more than £2.95. Other than the old slop, you can tuck into all sorts of other seafood as well as chicken and vegetarian fare. Make like a gangster's moll and chat about Chelsea smiles.

☻ *Tue–Sat, 11am–5pm*

⓫ *Jellied eels, £3*

The Sausage & Mash Café

4–6 Essex Road, N1

(020) 7359 5361

⊖ Angel

Have a desire for old-fashioned British home cooking, which your ill-equipped Home Economics skills just can't reach? Then head for the S & M cafe. At first glance it sounds a bit 'specialist' but actually it is a very accessible little café that serves up stonkingly good British food. Shepherds pie, all-day breakfasts and a huge variety of sausages (including wheat-free and organic), ensure an unlimited combination of dishes. Kitsch 50s Americana décor, reasonable prices and friendly service.

☻ *Mon–Sat, 7.30am–11.30pm; Sun, 7.30–10.30pm; Food, Mon–Sun, 7.30am–10.30pm*

⓫ *Sausage and Mash, £6.95*

ISLINGTON RESTAURANTS

Elk in the Woods

37 Camden Passage, N1

(020) 7226 3535

⊖ Angel

A bit of a hotch-potch of styles that manages to work, this place is definitely for the more upwardly mobile and a gang of antique trade regulars from Camden Passage. It's waiter service, which makes it perfect for those lazy evenings, and means the vibe is very relaxed. The food ranges from breakfast dishes to snacky platters and burgers. Pop a valium in the toilets and whisper a prayer to Barclaycard under your breath before you ask for the bill.

© *Mon–Sun, 10am-11pm*

ⓘ *Rich rabbit stew, £12.50*

Wagamama

40 Parkfield Street, N1

(020) 7226 2664

⊖ Angel

For reasonably priced, cheery and delicious Japanese food, Wagamama cannot be bettered. Even novices to this genre can find something they enjoy (and don't fear, chopsticks are not obligatory) in the range of noodles, sweet or sour soups and spicy or mild curries. A cosy atmosphere prevails, given the long-bench seating arrangements and constant hum of lots of satisfied customers – this place is always busy and for a very good reason. It's great. Go. 'Nuff said.

© *Mon–Sat, 12pm–11pm;*

Sun, 12.30pm–10pm

ⓘ *Chicken kare lomen, £7.25*

❷ *£10.95*

Gallipoli Bazaar

107 Upper Street, N1

(020) 7226 5333

⊖ Angel

This intimate and atmospheric Islington eatery offers a mouth–watering range of Turkish and Lebanese dishes, served by enthusiastic staff. Conversation is largely drowned out by the raucous music and the tables are vacuum-packed into a cramped and narrow space but if you don't mind banging elbows with the folks at the next table, you might even feel compelled to end the evening with a jubilant belly–dance on your table. More sheesha anyone?

© *Mon, closed; Tue, 5.30pm–11.30pm; Wed–Sat, 5.30pm–12pm; Sun, 12.30pm–11.30pm*

ⓘ *Bazaar meze, £6.95*

❷ *£10.95*

FINSBURY PARK

Faltering Fullback

19 Perth Road, N4

(020) 7272 5834

⇔ Finsbury Park

Some think that the Faltering Full Back is like a student's union for people who should know better. We tend to see that as a good thing, particularly when a cracking jukebox, tidy little beer garden, pool and table football are thrown into the equation. It can get really packed but that's a price you pay for somewhere in Finsbury Park with an atmosphere. Ideal for local drinks and relaxing with a pint on a summer's evening.

🕒 *Mon-Sat, 11am–11pm;*
Sun, 12pm–10.30pm

Jai Krishna

161 Stroud Green Road, N4

(020) 7272 1680

⇔ Finsbury Park

One of those places you can't quite believe still exists. With a school classroom ceiling, plastic seats and a treacherous outside toilet you're about as far from All Bar One as possible. Write down your own order, deliver it to the counter and await the arrival of an array of delicious and unusual vegetarian Indian food. The masala dosa is fantastic as is the jeer aloo – a house special potato dish. It's BYO so you can celebrate that special occasion with a nice bottle of Blue Nun.

🕒 *Mon-Sat, 12pm–2pm & 5.30pm–11pm*
🍴 *Masala dosa, £5*
🍷 *BYO*

Rowan's Bowling

10 Stroud Green Road, N4

(020) 8800 1950

⇔ Finsbury Park

Rowan's is a brilliant entertainment emporium for the young and the bored. At a quid to get in and a fiver for a game of ten pin bowling, you can always be tempted. Particularly when you can also get food, booze and dance to unfeasibly bad music until the early hours on the weekend. Imagine Missy Elliott bowling to a Shabba Ranks soundtrack and you're halfway there. Now, just prise yourself away from the X-Box (slowly, slowly) and go and do something vaguely physically improving instead.

🕒 *Fri–Sat, 10.30am-2.30am;*
Sun–Thu, 10.30am–12.30am

PRIMROSE HILL

Bartok

78–79 Chalk Farm Road, NW1

(020) 7916 0595

⊖ Chalk Farm

Late-drinking with a difference. Instead of being forced into a midnight lambada with a crusty rocker, you'll find cocktails, classical music and civilised girls called Charlotte and Claudia. Relax into the red interior, clink glasses and feel totally smug. Come the weekend they tend to pump up the volume and the place becomes a meat market for those with caviar tastes. No scrawny boys with bad haircuts here.

🕒 *Sun–Thu, 5pm–1am; Fri–Sat, 11am–2am*

🍴 *Nachos, £4.50*

💰 *£12.50*

The Queen's

49 Regent's Park Road, NW1

(020) 7586 0408

⊖ Camden Town/Chalk Farm

North London celebs love this place for its charming service and excellent gastro-style food. And that isn't to say that it's too good for you. Far from it: this place has never let us mere mortals down for a good feed and water. You're looking at restaurant prices for mains but the booze isn't marked up. Reward a day of Jude-stalking (sorry, we mean casual walking, ahem) on Primrose Hill with a bite and a few jars in here.

🕒 *Mon–Sat, 11am–11pm; Sun, 12pm–10.30pm; Food, Mon–Sat, 12pm–3pm & 7pm–10pm; Sun, 12.30pm–4pm & 7pm–9pm*

🍴 *Liver, bacon and mashed potato, £8.50*

Trojka

101 Regents Park Road, NW1

(020) 7483 3765

⊖ Chalk Farm

Although London's rich Russians like to come to Trojka for a taste of home, you don't need to be an oil-oligarch to eat here. Trojka serve up the best food from Russia with love, as well as typical Polish, Armenian, Ukrainian and Jewish dishes. If you are looking for somewhere to spend a fortune on caviar and blinis, you'll find the real thing here. They do a cracking breakfast, and if you need a little something to dull a hangover, you could do worse than a shot of their excellent vodka.

🕒 *Mon–Sun, 9am 'til late*

🍴 *Polish pork sausage with sauerkraut, goulash and mash, £7*

North

KING'S CROSS

The Cross, The Key and Canvas
King's Cross Depot, N1
(020) 7837 1027
⊖ King's Cross

This trio of King's Cross clubs play dance music until the early hours, providing good reasons to negotiate York Way at truly ridiculous times of day or night. The Key is home to messy electro-house nights like 'All Over My Face' and 'Foreign Muck', while the Cross hosts upmarket (read: expensive) house institutions like 'Type' and 'Fiction'. So, the Key gets the clubbers, the Cross gets the posers… and Canvas is the place to go if you fancy a roller disco. On Saturdays, Canvas hosts an ever-changing range of parties.
Ⓒ *Thu–Sat, 10pm–6am*

Ruby Lounge
33 Caledonian Road, N1
(020) 7837 9558
⊖ King's Cross

Very much a DJ bar, which is handily close to King's Cross, the clientele are young and fashionable and music is very much for people who talk about 'the groove' and 'the funk'. Pete Tong described it as his favourite bar in London so read into that what you will. What we do know is that the DJs are sharp, the atmosphere laid back and the cocktails excellent with little of the snobbery of a similar place in the West End. Plus you can even sit out on the pavement in the summer sun. Mmmm... inhale that smog.
Ⓒ *Mon-Thu, 4pm-11pm; Sat, 4pm-2am; Sun, 4pm-10.30pm*

Scala
275 Pentonville Road, N1
(020) 7833 2022
⊖ King's Cross

Four floors of fun for up to 1,000 people. Set in an old theatre, Scala is one of London's most opulent venues and also one of its most eclectic. With everything from cutting-edge dance music to random Latino festival offerings, there has to be something here for you. Regular nights include 'Kill All Hippies' and the gay, indie love-fest that is 'Popstarz', while the live stage has recently been graced by the likes of Kruder & Dorfmeister, The Scissor Sisters and The Foo Fighters. You'll have to join the humungous queue, but it really is worth standing out in the cold for.
Ⓒ *Fri-Sat, 10pm-5am*

GET INTO THE GROOVE

'I BET THAT YOU LOOK GOOD ON THE DANCEFLOOR', SING THE ARCTIC MONKEYS.
JUDGING BY THE SHAMBOLIC MOVES ON MOST CITY CENTRE DANCEFLOORS,
THEY LOST THAT BET. FOLLOW THE GUIDE TO SHAKIN' YOUR ASS LIKE ITCHY, AND
PREPARE TO BE THE TALK OF THE TOWN (FOR ALL THE RIGHT REASONS).

Illustration by Anja Wohlstrom

1. **The Travolta**
   Reach for the sky and reclaim
   this classic from yer dad.
2. **Hand spin**
   Twirl those legs like a castrato.
3. **Step and clap**
   This simple move served Rick
   Astley well in the 80s, so nick
   it for the noughties.

East

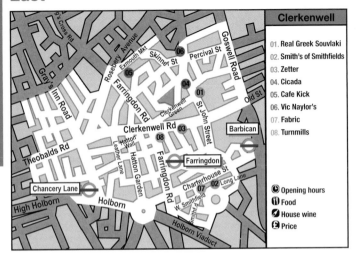

Clerkenwell

01. Real Greek Souvlaki
02. Smith's of Smithfields
03. Zetter
04. Cicada
05. Cafe Kick
06. Vic Naylor's
07. Fabric
08. Turnmills

🕐 Opening hours
🍴 Food
🍷 House wine
💲 Price

CLERKENWELL BARS

Al's Bar

11–13 Exmouth Market, EC1
(020) 7837 4821
🚇 Farringdon

For when you have to pack as much hangover removing grease as possible into your system, Al's Bar is the place to head. The breakfasts are legendary, and in the summer, the outdoor seating makes it an ideal mood–lifting place. And if you're only really trying to shift the hangover, you could do a lot worse than spend the coming evening in Al's too. Crowds ram this late–licensed bar to shake their funky thing on the downstairs dance floor, Just a shame you can't sleep there too.

🕐 *Mon–Tue, 8am–11pm; Wed–Fri, 8am–2am; Sat, 10am–2am; Sun, 10am–11pm*

Café Kick

43 Exmouth Market, EC1
(020) 7837 8077
🚇 Angel/Farringdon

The kind of bar that takes you back in time to your gap year, and the happy nights you spent sleeping in French youth hostels, choking on Gauloises and rubbing up against girls called Estelle. Cafe Kick could be anywhere in Europe with its table-footy theme and wine served in glass beakers. That's as far as the similarities go though, so hopefully your chat up technique has moved on a little from offering a bite of your sausage. Times have changed, Monsieur Love Machine.

🕐 *Mon–Sat, 12pm–11pm;*
Sun, 5pm–10.30pm
🍴 *Bean and cured ham salad, £5.50*
🍷 *£12*

Cicada

132–136 St John Street, EC1

(020) 7608 1550

⊖ Farringdon

Catering for trendy advertising types, this roomy and modern. There's a great range of cocktails and the food is superb, drawing on Thai, Vietnamese, Chinese and Japanese influences. The downstairs 'red room' is available for hire, and with decks installed you'll want your party right here. It's pretty much a 19th-century style Chinese opium den, complete with Chinese lanterns, and a dragon painted on the front of the bar. Be warned however that the restaurant area is often fully booked, so it's worth reserving a table.

◉ *Mon–Fri, 12pm–11pm; Sat, 6pm–11pm; Sun, closed*

Hat on Wall

24–28 Hatton Wall, EC1

(020) 7242 9939

⊖ Farringdon

Still the best hidden arts bar in London. It's members only but honestly, trust us, as long as you're not with ten sombrero-clad rugby lads, they'll let you in. Once you're through the pearly gates – go through the entrance to Black Bull Yard, up the stairs and you'll find it through the doors on the first floor – you'll find an artfully wasted crowd sipping vodka tonics in time to the DJ's latest music fad. This is a top place to hire for a party – for £100 you can have the place to yourself.

◉ *Wed–Sat, 6ish–latish*

Match

45–47 Clerkenwell Road, EC1

(020) 7250 4002

⊖ Farringdon

Delicious, colourful, but pricey cocktails and an abundance of office chicks. As a result, men seem to flock here - the kind of men that call girls 'ladies' and not in a jokey way, but don't seem to mind getting their gold cards out in return for the pleasure of their company. That all sounds a bit negative but it isn't intended to be. Match is a classy venue that inspires the kind of night out that ends in tequilas all round and a dodgy taxi home.

◉ *Mon–Fri, 11am–12am; Sat, 5pm–12am*

◙ *Champagne cocktails, £6.75*

East

Meet

85 Charterhouse Street, EC1

(020) 7490 5790

⊖ Farringdon

It's not the size of your shaker that counts, it's what you do with it. The team at Meet take the art of creating drinks to a new level. Forget curly straws or spinning bottles round your head, all these guys care about is making delicious drinks for you using the very best ingredients they can find. They'll even ask you how you're feeling before they serve you to make sure your drink fits your mood. Can it get any better? At around £5.50 per cocktail, the prices aren't as high as you'd imagine, so take a sip, lie back, and think of England.

☺ Mon–Wed, 11am–1am; Thu–Sat, 11am–4am; Sun, 11am–12pm

Vic Naylors

38/40 St John Street, EC1

(020) 7608 2181

⊖ Farringdon

It's the *Lock Stock* bar with candles, swanky red curtains and leather booths, and it's a top place for a few relaxing beers. There's lots of after work drinkers but enough trainers to make sure it's not overrun with suits. They play good tunes and it doesn't get too rammed. But there's an annoying lack of draught beer and a £10 minimum on your card. The seating could be better too; booths only seat five, max – and there's usually a smoochy couple hogging one. We wonder if they do ice buckets?

☺ Mon, 12pm–12am; Tue–Fri, 12pm–1am; Sat, 6pm–1am

CLERKENWELL PUBS

Jerusalem Tavern

55 Britton Street, EC1

(020) 7490 4281

⊖ Farringdon

This tiny spot is easy to miss unless you know it's there, hiding itself away from the clatter of Farringdon hot-spots nearby. Word's spreading quickly however, as the bar is often full with beer-loving twenty-something's eager to try whatever special's been trucked in from St Peter's brewery in Suffolk. Almost like drinking with farmers, in London, without the farmers. The candles and tiled décor make this a romantic treat if you don't mind the limited room, or standing when it gets busy.

☺ Mon–Sat, 12pm–11pm; Sun, 12pm–10.30pm

CLERKENWELL CLUBS

Fabric

77a Charterhouse Street, EC1

(020) 7336 8898

⊖ Farringdon

You can stand outside with a sandwich board and a megaphone and scream, 'Death to the superclub' 'til your eyes burst, but the kids ain't giving up on Fabric yet. Always a cut-above, whatever way you look at it, this baby's got it going on. Try Fridays' 'Fabric Live' for the likes of Unkle and Nicky Blackmarket or Saturday's full-on bleeding-edge house night. They'll have you putting your hands in the air and waving them like you just don't care in no time.

◉ *Fri, 9.30pm–5am; Sat, 10pm–7am*

Turnmill's

63b Clerkenwell Road, EC1

(020) 7250 3409

⊖ Farringdon

Still flying the flag high for house and techno obsessives with a blend of cutting-edge and old-time classic nights. Try Friday's 'Gallery' with mix-masters such as Paul Oakenfold, Sister Bliss, Tall Paul, Steve Lee and Pete Tong on the case or Saturday's varied nights (City Loud, Smartie Partie, Together and Love Box on rotate). Also worth a butcher's is the top floor bar, which serves swanky breakfasts (so you can give the greasy spoon a miss) and dinner in a slick lounge environment.

◉ *Thu, 9pm–3am; Fri, 10.30pm–7.30am; Sat, 10pm–7am; Sun, 10pm–5am*

East

CLERKENWELL RESTAURANTS

Medcalf

40 Exmouth Market, EC1

(020) 7833 3533

⊖ Farringdon/Angel

A nearly new bar/pub/restaurant/café with an airy, rough-and-ready feel. There's something for most tastes with early-morning coffees, DJs at weekends, plenty of wines to glug your way through and utterly pleasant staff. We're fully loving the place with its buzz and boho stragglers.

◉ Mon–Fri, 10am–11pm; Sat, 7pm–11pm; Sun, 12pm–10.30pm; Food, Mon–Thu 10am–9pm; Fri, 10am–8pm; Sun, 12pm–5pm

🆔 Salt cod fritters with tartare sauce, £3.95

❷ £12

Quality Chop House

94 Farringdon Road, EC1

(020) 7837 5093

⊖ Farringdon

This, so they tell us, is a 'progressive working class caterer'. Now what that effectively means is that is used to be the kind of place builders could go to fill up on cheap butties and now it's so expensive only middle class business-types can foot the bill. If that's progress then so be it. Food-wise, it's great and uses high-quality ingredients to cook up British classics. Take your Gran next time she's in town.

◉ Mon–Fri, 12pm–3pm; Mon–Sat, 6.30pm–11.30pm; Sun, 12pm–4pm & 7pm–11.30pm

🆔 Beef and Guinness sausages with mashed potato, £9.95

❷ £12.95

Real Greek Souvlaki Bar

140–142 St John Street, EC1

(020) 7253 7234

⊖ Farringdon

Enjoy a kebab minus the ten-pint hangover for once. Souvlaki Bar, from the folks behind the Real Greek in Hoxton, offers a lesson for the as yet unenlightened in how good meat and pitta can actually be. Taste the difference, weep over years of wasted opportunity and clink glasses of Greek champagne (love the old-fashioned glasses) in celebration of the fact that your greasy, cold doner days are now long behind you. Also good for mezze and drinks in the spacious industrial style bar.

◉ Mon–Sat, 10am–11pm

🆔 Grilled pork cutlets, £5.90

❷ £11.55

Smiths of Smithfields

67–77 Charterhouse Street, EC1

(020) 7251 7950

⊖ Farringdon

A short walk from Farringdon, this is the place to be seen and you're looked up and down as soon as you walk through the door. The ground floor is a darkened, bustling hive of wine drinkers bearing the latest trends as they huddle round massive tables. Upstairs the swish-looking NYC style bar serves a fab cocktail and the restaurants (the top floor being amazing but expensive, the other being moderately priced but yummy) are both always busy.

🕙 *Daily, 7am–11pm*

🍴 *Risotto with macadamia nuts, £11.75*

💰 *£12.75*

St John Bread and Wine

94–96 Commercial Street, E1

(020) 7247 8724

⊖ Aldgate East

Not a place for the squeamish, this. Specialising in 'nose to tail' eating, chef Fergus Henderson creates a menu out of the parts of animals that most people leave behind. This cheaper cousin of pricier St John affords plenty of options for those who prefer a more traditional approach to food though, and it's worth a trip just to say you've been, if nothing else. Plus you won't suffer the indignity of paying top whack for the cheapest parts of animals, unlike at the other branch.

🕙 *Mon–Fri, 9am–11pm; Sat, 10am–11pm; Sun, 10am–6pm*

🍴 *Old Spot bacon sandwich, £4.80*

💰 *£14.50*

Zetter

86 Clerkenwell Road, EC1

(020) 7324 4455

⊖ Farringdon

The hotel is already known as one of the hippest in the world, and we think the restaurant is just as good. Make up an occasion, propose if you have to (you can always back out later), just make sure you find a reason to make this restaurant the venue for your next meal. The bar is equally fabulous and filled with impossibly cool people being, well, fabulous. If even an ounce of what they've got going on here rubs off on you, you'll be hot property.

🕙 *Mon–Fri, 7am–10.30am & 12pm–2.30pm & 6pm–11pm; Sat, 7.30am–3pm & 6pm–11pm; Sun, 7.30am–3pm & 6pm–10.30pm*

🍴 *Grilled seabass with salsa verde, £17*

💰 *£11*

East

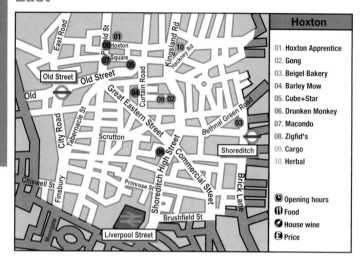

HOXTON BARS

Big Chill

Dray Walk, E1
(07870) 339 509
⊖ Liverpool Street/Shoreditch

The crowd are what you'd expect for this corner of London: we're talking Hoxton wasters and muso types comparing trainers and i-Pod playlists over their pints. Summer is the business, with DJs, plenty of outside seating and a constant stream of pretty folk walking past to keep the people-watchers happy. There's nowhere finer for weekend time-wasting round this part of town.

◷ Mon–Sat, 12pm–12am; Sun, 12pm–11.30pm; Food, Mon–Sun, 12pm–11pm
🍴 Steak ciabatta with chimi churri salsa, £6.50
🍷 £11

Cube & Star

39a Hoxton Square, N1
(020) 7739 8824
⊖ Old Street

If you want to know where the Shoreditch twits of the nineties now hang-out, look no further than this yuppie palace. The Electricity Showrooms closed and was reborn as this cocktail lounge / restaurant / jazz club. Hoxton used to stand for edgy cool, (cue crazy hair, bargain beers and bars with no names), but now it has places with clever names serving quality food and drinks at a price. Bad news for those with funny haircuts. Great news for those wanting to impress a date.

◷ Mon–Thu, 11am–12pm; Fri–Sat, 11am–1am; Sun, 11am–11pm
🍴 4 tapas dishes for £12
🍷 £11.50

Dragon Bar

Leonard Street, EC2

(020) 7490 7110

⊖ Old Street

This place has all the makings of a pretentious montrosity – with its reputation for being 'secret', uber-trendy music, a shoreditch location and faux street-chic interior. However, this is probably one of the best bars in London. The atmosphere is relaxing to the point of hypnotisation. There's almost always a pretty young lady playing funk, hip-hop or reggae on the decks. The clientele are an altogether less annoying breed of Hoxditch trendies, and the staff, for a change, don't resent your existence.

Ⓒ *Mon–Sat, 11am–11pm;*
Sun, 12pm–10.30pm

Ⓐ *£14*

Lounge Lover

1 Whitby Street, E1

(020) 7012 1234

⊖ Shoreditch/Old Street/Bethnal Green

For girls who want an excuse to dress up, and boys who want to undress them, Lounge Lover is the business. Décor is opulent – giant champagne glasses filled with flowers, eternal flame torches, pouffes and porn and mirrors – you'll feel like you've shrunk, dropped some acid and ended up at Elton John's house on Eurovision night. Make a booking in advance; though if they're quiet they'll find a space for you. Swot up on fancy cocktails and be prepared to shell out a small fortune.

Ⓒ *Tue–Sat, 6pm–12am; Food, Tue–Sat,*
6.30pm–10.30pm

Ⓜ *Ostrich steak with vegetables, £16.50*

Ⓐ *£18*

Drunken Monkey

222 Shoreditch High Street, E1

(020) 7392 9606

⊖ Liverpool Street/Old Street

What rave reviews give with one hand they take away with the other. Drunken Monkey was busy settling into its low-key Shoreditch High Street location when it was nominated for an Evening Standard award; the tills haven't stopped ringing since. Good news for whoever rubs their hands over the takings, bad for E1 locals who hadn't got round to a visit yet. During the week the original vibe remains, but come the weekend it's suits-by-the-dozen and pumping bass.

Ⓒ *Mon–Fri, 12pm–12am; Sat, 6pm–12am;*
Sun, 12pm–12am

Ⓜ *Roast duck and rice, £5.50*

Ⓐ *£12.50*

East

Macondo

8–9 Hoxton Square, N1

(020) 7729 1119

⊖ Old Street

Macondo is a cosy space (Ok, cramped) but there is something likeable about this fairly narrow room and its hodge-podge of furniture (leather sofas, poofs and even a wicker egg chair suspended from the ceiling). Maybe it's the fact that every surface has some kind of goodie on it. Cake-stands sit aloft shelves with all the traditionals', (lemon drizzle, coffee and walnut and Victoria sponge), as do bowls of olives. Cocktails are about £6–7 while cakes are £3 a wodge and food (quesadillas, tortillas) are around £6.

🕒 *Sun–Thu, 9.30am–11pm; Fri–Sat, 9.30am–12am*

🍴 *Nachos, £5.95*

💰 *£13.50*

Zigfrid

11 Hoxton Square, N1

(020) 7613 1988

⊖ Old Street

Paul Daly's bar venture isn't bad per se, but if there ever was a venue that came straight off the 'How to build a Hoxton bar' production line, this was it. It's spacious and arty with a random array of furniture. Punters are posh girls from Fulham slumming it out east. There's outside seating looking onto the square and decent Brit-dish style food. There are banging tunes at weekends and bottled beers called 'Coq'. All very 'done before' and uninspiring. He did a lovely job on the Hoxton Apprentice across the road though.

🕒 *Mon–Sat, 12pm–12am; Sun, 12pm–11pm*

🍴 *Roast peppers and gorgonzola salad, £6.50*

💰 *£10.50*

HOXTON PUBS

Barley Mow

127 Curtain Road, EC2

(020) 7729 3910

⊖ Old Street

No nonsense in the Barley Mow. No sir. Grab a picnic table outside or huddle together on the in, order a pint and assemble a few mates. If you tune out meditation-stylee and don't look at the passing trade, you could be just about anywhere. In this part of town that's a good thing. Tuck into some crisps, ask your mate about his redundancy package and discuss re-runs of Friends. Make like the Hoxton Fin was never invented.

🕒 *Mon–Thu, 12pm–11pm; Fri, 12pm–12am; Sat, 2pm–12am; Sun, 2pm–10.30pm*

HOXTON CLUBS

Cargo

83 Rivington Street, EC2

(020) 7739 3440

⊖ Old Street

Another star of the scene with an impressive roll-call of live acts, top-quality nights and the best outdoor space in Hoxton. Whether you're tucking into burgers in the Street Soul Café, chilling out back with a beer or throwing your arms in the air like you don't have to go to work in the morning, Cargo is a mighty choice of nightspot to throw your cash at. We'd expect no less from the genius behind Hoxton stalwart Cantaloupe and central London's Market Place.

ⓒ *Mon–Wed, 12pm–1am; Fri, 12pm–3am; Sat, 12pm–3am; Sun, 12pm–12am*

Mother/333

333 Old Street, EC1

(020) 7739 5949

⊖ Old Street

Once one of those 'little place I know' deals, now sporting decidedly non-exclusive banner style signage. Don't let this put you off – Mother Bar still has what it takes to make the kids happy. On any given night of the week this is the only place round here that's guaranteed to be full to bursting – Brazilian students will be dancing alongside Alexander McQueen and the DJ will be playing Joan Jett's *I love Rock'n'Roll*. Check out Tuesday nights Grubby Rock'n'Roll – punky garage for the midweek freak contingent. If you can't beat 'em...

ⓒ *Mon–Sun, 8pm–2am*

Herbal

12–14 Kingsland Road, EC2

(020) 7613 4462

⊖ Old Street

Still pulling 'em in for a spectrum of quality nights. And still getting it right with Sunday sessions, a pretension-free atmosphere and plenty of innovative new stuff in the mix. There's a rough-and-ready but comfortable feel to the place, a buzz of excitement and a small enough capacity to mean you don't spend half your night chatting to freaks in the toilets. It's a bit of a schlep up Kingsland Road, but you'll be glad you skipped a little further away from the Chloe Sevigny looky-likies.

ⓒ *Thu, 9pm–2am; Fri, 9pm–3am; Sat, 9pm–3am; Sun, 9pm–2am*

East

Lennie's

6 Calvert Avenue, EC1

(020) 7739 3628

⊖ Old Street

A fry-up caff by day and bizarrely romantic Thai eatery by night, Lennie's takes some beating. Rock up for a ramshackle evening of candlelight and banter with the owner. She'll cook up a bit of whatever you fancy, depending on what ingredients she has left at the time. Plus there's free entertainment by way of regaled tales of Hoxtonian hilarity.

🕐 *Mon, 6am–4pm; Tue–Sat, 6am–4pm & 7pm–12am; Sun, 10am–2pm*

🍴 *Spicy chicken curried noodles, £5*

💰 *BYO*

Fifteen Trattoria

15 Westland Place, N1

(0871) 330 1515

⊖ Old Street

Take a dollop of Italian-inspired cooking, add a selection of beaudeeful fresh produce, mash up with a splash of altruism, and bish, bash, bosh, you have the Trattoria at Fifteen. And after chowing down on the tasty, rustic cooking, the friendly service and buzzing atmosphere'll have you exclaiming 'Pukka!' with as much enthusiasm as the gurning mockney tool himself. Lovely-jubbly.

🕐 *Mon–Sat 12–3pm & 6–10pm*

🍴 *Seaside risotto with saffron and fennel, £14*

💰 *£20*

Gong

65 Rivington Street, EC2

(020) 7033 2974

⊖ Old Street

'Red and yellow and blue and green, purple and orange and pink. I can sing a rainbow…' These are the words that you may find yourself uttering in response to the fact that in the middle of Gong's black and white, minimalist décor, lies a wall that changes through all the colours of the rainbow. Alternatively, you might find yourself joining the clientele of Hoxton trendies raving about Guangbo Tang, the award-winning chef's creative line in Dim-Sum centric Chinese, Japanese and Thai cuisine.

🕒 *Mon–Sun, 12pm–3pm & 6pm–12pm*

🍴 *Dim sum selection, £15 (for two)*

💷 *£12.50*

Hoxton Apprentice

16 Hoxton Square, N1

(020) 7749 2828

⊖ Old Street

This modern dining space set on two floors looks majestic. French windows make up the front of this grand, high-vaulted space (the first overlooks the ground floor effectively doubling the height of the room). Food is served in small or large portions and is simply divine, while the good wine list is concise and excellently priced. Staff are consistently superb and even better the restaurant has been set-up by a charity and employs the unemployed/homeless.

🕒 *Tue–Sat, 12pm–11pm*

🍴 *Goat's cheese, sweet potato and red onion tart, £6.99*

💷 *£11.50*

Hoxton Bar and Kitchen

2–4 Hoxton Square, N1

(020) 7613 1171

⊖ Old Street

This dimly lit bar in the heart of Nathan Barley land is furnished with a number of beaten-up 70s leather sofas, tea-lights, simple low tables and dominated by a long granite bar. Due to the size of the place (big enough for cat-swinging Olympics) it never gets that smoky. There didn't seem to be that many people eating when we showed up, but prices are about average and the staff pleasant enough.

🕒 *Mon–Thu, 11am–12am; Fri–Sat, 11am–2am; Sun, 12pm–12am*

🍴 *Beef Wellington, £14*

💷 *£11.50*

East

BRICK LANE

Beigel Bakery

159 Brick Lane, E1

(020) 7729 0616

⊖ Shoreditch/Liverpool Street/Old Street

What do the angels eat after a heavy night in the pub? Simple. A freshly baked salt-beef bagel with plenty of English mustard. But where, we hear you ask, do they go for that? Well, they come to the East End, because on Brick Lane, they can get a bagel anytime of day or night, on any day of the year. Divine stuff, at earthly prices. And apparently the number 8 bus stops right outside the pearly gates, so they don't have to get a mini-cab home.

ⓒ *Daily, 24 hours*

ⓘ *Salt-beef beigel, £2.10*

The Golden Heart

110 Commercial Street, E1

(020) 7247 2158

⊖ Liverpool Street

Bloody fantastic. The Golden Heart may have made it onto the radar of London's cool-stalkers but the regulars don't seem to have noticed. Inside you'll find old boys clinking glasses with Japanese fashion students and a jukebox playing Frank Sinatra. Landlady Sandra is a fan of the ad-hoc tap dance and knows how to sort the wheat from the chaff. Potential trouble is danced out the door with a nod from the glass collector on exit. Tracy Emin has been known to pull a few pints and throw some shapes in here. A fine boozer that'll never lose its old-skool feel. We'll drink to that.

ⓒ *Mon–Fri, 1am-11pm; Sun, 11am-10.30pm*

New Tayyabs

83 Fieldgate Street

(020) 7247 9543

⊖ Whitechapel

If you're sick of Brick Lane not coming up to scratch this palace of Pakistani delights will re-light your fire. Waiters are ten-a-penny and hectic and devoid of manners, punters are post-mosque locals and student layabouts. Meat-fans should order lamb chops (trust us or check out the marinades at the back) and veggies will be happy with fiery chick-pea or spinach karahis. Naans are buttery and rotis are massive, bubbly and freshly made. BYO booze or go local style with a jug of water. Amazing.

ⓒ *Mon–Sun, 5pm–11.30pm*

ⓑ *BYO*

BETHNAL GREEN

The Dove

24 Broadway Market, E8

(020) 7275 7617

⊖ Bethnal Green

If you're down on the East End canal at Broadway Market, you'll no doubt succumb to the charms of the Dove from above. The 120 beers on offer, complement the Dove's specialty beer-marinated gourmet sausages and burgers, and the monthly beer and cheese nights will seal the deal. And just between you and us – take in a bar of Dairy Milk, order a glass of Leffe Brun and prepare to have a mouth orgasm.

☺ *Mon–Thu, 12pm–11pm; Fri–Sat, 12pm–12am; Sun, 10.30pm*

🍴 *Burger, £5.95*

The Florist

255 Globe Road, E2

(020) 8981 1100

⊖ Bethnal Green

What do you get when you call a pub a florist? A damn good pub! In place of the tulips and petunias are a wide range of beers and spirits, and posh pub nibbles, including great olives. The homegrown Eastenders mix with the young and artsy at comedian-hosted quiz nights and the infamous open-deck Sundays. And if you get peckish, nip next door to the Florists' sibling boozer, the Camel, for homemade gourmet pie and mash in a smoke-free and cosy bistro setting. Now, that's what we call the easy life.

☺ *Mon–Fri, 2.30pm–11pm; Sat, 12pm–11pm; Sun, 12pm–10.30pm*

The Palm Tree

Haverfield Road, E3

(020) 8890 2918

⊖ Mile End

Hidden away in a nest of trees (three of which are palm trees) a few steps off the canal path near Mile End lies an old-school pub you won't miss on a Friday, Saturday or Sunday night. That's when the elderly crooners come out to play and treat ears old and young with the classics, sung live to the piano. On these nights, when the faded curtains are closed and the reasonably priced beer is flowing, it's like stepping back in time to when pubs were real social clubs for all ages.

☺ *Mon–Sat, 12pm–11pm; Sun, 12pm–10.30pm*

East

Coq d'Argent

No 1 Poultry, EC2

(020) 7395 5000

⊖ Bank

Coq d'Argent is a rooftop oasis, with views across town from the lawn. Yes, you did read that right. Mr Conran has laid a lawn and installed a veritable hanging garden of Babylon. They also provide rugs, for elaborate picnicking or decorous draping. This kind of luxury doesn't come cheap, but if ever there was a reason to go trawling for a sugar daddy, this place is it. Alternatively, take a date and a black Amex, and contemplate the phallic significance of the Gherkin.

🕓 *Open: Mon–Fri, 7.30am–10am, 11.30am–3pm & 6pm–10pm; Sun, 12pm–3pm*

🍴 *Two courses, £23*

🍷 *£13.50*

The Counting House

50 Cornhill, EC3

(020) 7283 7123

⊖ Bank

Buy! Sell! Go Tokyo! As you can well imagine, this place is full of bankers. (We said 'bankers'.) Mind you, here at Itchy we like to posh it up every now and again, so put on your dad's pinstripe suit and make haste to cash centrale. This pub used to be a bank, and the place is still dripping with the trappings of wealth. There are chandeliers and ornate mouldings all over the shop. We think there's something deliciously perverse about pissing your wages straight up the wall in an ex-bank.

🕓 *Mon–Fri, 11am–11pm; Sat–Sun, closed*

🍴 *Sunday roast, £5.75*

🍷 *£10.25*

Silks & Spice

11 Queen Victoria Street

(020) 7248 7878

⊖ Blackfriars

Decent Thai/Malay food in a restaurant that caters well to big groups and parties. The overheard gossip on our visit was totally unprintable – put it this way the city ladies eating out here don't have much in the way of boundaries. It's like an episode of Sex and the City but with more briefcases. Not bad value either. If you want a Tom Yum soup so fresh and fierce that one sip feels like it can cure TB, come here.

🕓 *Mon–Tue, 11.30am–11pm; Wed, 11.30am–11.30pm; Thu–Fri, 11.30am–2am*

🍴 *Tom Kha Kai, 4.75*

🍷 *£10*

FISH AND CHIPS

MOST OF THE CAPITAL'S CHIPPIES LEAVE A LOT TO BE DESIRED, BUT GETTING YOUR FILL OF THE NATIONAL DISH IN LONDON DOESN'T HAVE TO BE BASED AROUND LIMP CHIPS AND GREYING WEEK OLD SLICES OF COD. READ ON FOR ITCHY'S SELECTION OF THE FEW PLACES THAT, WHEN THE CHIPS WERE DOWN, WEREN'T LEFT FISHING FOR COMPLIMENTS.

Rock and Sole Plaice

47 Endell Street, WC2

⊖ Covent Garden

Since being taken over by new ownership, London's oldest fish and chip shop may be a far cry from its glory days, but it's still a chip off the old block (ahem). The selection of fish is one of the widest the capital has to offer, with the likes of mackerel, skate and tuna steak sitting alongside the standard chippie range of cod, pies and saveloys.

Fishcotheque

79a Waterloo Road, SE1

⊖ Waterloo

It may be nestled under one of the capital's grottiest bridges, but avoid the hail of pigeon faeces from overhead and nip inside for a good helping of thick–cut chips. Fish is fried fresh daily, and being near a major train station, there's always a good cross–section of London society bustling in and out. Acquaint yourself with the locals as you munch.

Fryer's Delight

19 Theobald's Road, WC1

⊖ Holborn

Veggies beware: you'll struggle to find anything here that hasn't been fried in beef dripping. But for the die-hard chippy fans amongst you, this is fish and chips as its best. Plonk yourself down at one of the tables in this no–frills and listen to one of this restaurant's cabby clientele reeling off a list of the various Z-listers they've overcharged over the years.

Two Brothers Fish Restaurant

303 Regent's Park Road, N3

⊖ Finchley Central

For the health conscious looking for a chippy (odd, but possible), this is the place. Not only does the restaurant's policy of no smoking in the evening spare your lungs, but the fact that fish comes steamed as well as battered means that you don't need to worry about piling on the pounds. Until you start to lard out on the chips, that is.

CHAT-UP LINES

THANKS TO ITCHY, YOU NEVER HAVE TO GO HOME ALONE. HOWEVER, PLEASE BE AWARE THAT WE TAKE NO RESPONSIBILITY FOR YOUR ACTIONS AFTERWARDS.

– 'The word of the day is 'legs'. Let's go back to my place and spread the word.'

– 'Your eyes are like spanners... Every time you look at me my nuts tighten.'

– Break a bit of ice on the bar and say, 'Now I've broken the ice can I buy you a drink?'

– 'You remind me of a parking ticket. Because you've got 'fine' written all over you.'

– 'Are you wearing mirrored pants? (They say no.) Funny, because I can see myself in them.'

– 'Hi, I'm Mr Right. Someone said you were looking for me.'

– 'What's the name of that hot, black drink they sell in Starbucks?' (They reply, 'Coffee'). 'Sure. Your place or mine?'

– 'Will you help me find my lost puppy? I think he just went into a cheap hotel room over the road.'

– 'Do you like animals? Because I'm a real wildcat when you get to know me.'

– 'Have you just farted? Because you've blown me away.'

– 'I'm no Fred Flintstone, but I can sure make your bed rock.'

– 'Shag me if I'm wrong, but haven't we met before?'

– Do you play the trumpet? Only you're making me horny.

Illustration by Ben Anderson-Bauer

South

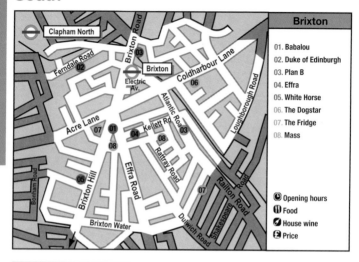

Brixton

01. Babalou
02. Duke of Edinburgh
03. Plan B
04. Effra
05. White Horse
06. The Dogstar
07. The Fridge
08. Mass

🕐 Opening hours
🍴 Food
🍷 House wine
💷 Price

BRIXTON BARS

Babalou

The Crypt, St Matthew's Church, SW2
(0207) 738 3366
⊖ Brixton

Unless you're Cliff Richard, your idea of a good Friday night out is unlikely to involve going to a church. Except if you come to Babalou, that is. Its reasonably priced modern cuisine and signature cocktails are currently providing South London's air-kissers with a reason to spend a night in a crypt. Just don't expect to be able to hear your dinner companions' conversation over the sound system.

🕐 *Restaurant, Wed–Sun, 6pm–11pm;*
Bar/Club, Wed–Thu, 5pm–2am; Fri–Sat,
5pm–6am; Sun, 5pm–11pm

Brixtonian Havana Bar

11 Beehive Place, SW9
(020) 7924 9262
⊖ Brixton

There's an air of mystery about this place, perfect for hot dates or nights out where you don't intend to remember much about the whole affair in the morning. With a backyard bar for al fresco sipping and chilling, this is a Brixton stalwart that's gone the distance. Try 'Heatwave', a monthly Saturday dancehall night or 'Full Menu' (Thursdays) for soulful house and reggae. Alternatively make your own fun with a hedonistic trip through the cocktail menu: The Brixton Riot is legendary.

🕐 *Mon–Thu, 12pm–1am; Fri–Sat,*
12pm–2am; Sun, 12pm–12am;
Food, Mon–Wed, 7pm–10.30pm
💷 *£14.95*

Bug Bar

St Matthews Church, Brixton Hill, SW2

(020) 7738 3366

⊖ Brixton

Bug practically invented the DJ bar concept and is still going as strong as when it first opened. It's big though and despite a loungey makeover it can still feel like you're drinking alone in a dungeon on a quiet night. Still, come Thursday it's buzzing. Punters are a mix of thrill-seeking tourists, locals reliving the old days and diners from the adjoining (and fabulous) restaurant. With DJs playing old school house, hip hop and RnB and the odd live gig there's plenty to keep you amused down here.

☻ *Tue–Thu, 7pm–11pm& 12am; Fri–Sat, 8pm–3am; Sun, 7pm–2am; Food, Tue–Sun, 5pm–11pm*

Plan B

418 Brixton Road, SW2

(0870) 1165 421

⊖ Brixton

This is the spot to watch B-Boys battling it out on the mic, or get your groove on to a decent DJ. Plan B is not the kind of place you drop into after work for a quiet drink, although there's a 2-4-1 happy hour (on selected cocktails and beers) every night until 9pm. It's a party spot designed for poppin' and lockin', two-stepping and covert dance voyeurism for the rhythmically challenged.

☻ *Tue–Wed, 5pm–12am; Thu, 5pm–2am; Fri, 5pm–4am; Sat, 7pm–4am*

❂ *Happy hour until 9pm every day*

Redstar

319 Camberwell Road, SE5

(0871) 3326 424

⊖ Oval/Denmark Hill (BR)

Thank the good Lord for Redstar. It treads the fine line between fun and fondue, and guarantees a riotous night out. There's a massive beer garden out the front – a real punter-puller in summer – and inside you'll find an expanse of dancefloor big enough for the most ambitious head-spin. Music spans the decades time forgot and by midnight everyone is on the floor; lip-synching Britney-style into a microphone made out of a straw.

☻ *Mon–Thu, 5pm–2am; Fri–Sat, 5pm–4am; Sun, 5pm–12am*

South

BRIXTON PUBS

Duke of Edinburgh

204 Ferndale Road, SW9

(020) 7924 0509

⊖ Brixton

The biggest beer garden in the whole of South London. Fact. We haven't been out there with a trundle wheel or anything, but we reckon we're on the mark. If it's summer and you're up for a pint, we recommend you start a queue the night before. Take a picnic – it'll be just like that time you camped outside Gary Barlow's nan's house. Your keenness will be rewarded as you perch at a picnic table and sneer at the standing hordes of red-faced tourists.

🕒 *Mon–Sat, 12pm–11pm; Sun, 1pm–10.30pm; Food, Mon–Sun, 6pm–9.30pm*

Effra Hall

38 Kellet Road, SW2

(020) 7274 4180

⊖ Brixton

Everyone loves this bohemian Victorian boozer and well they might. Clientele are so devoted, most of them have their own arse prints in the furniture, but they're a pretty welcoming bunch. Join local celebrities, musos and slow-drinking old men for pool, jazz, reggae and a pint in the beer garden. This is a spot-on boozer for anyone who's sick to the back teeth of the techno crowd, so it's probably best to leave your glo-sticks at home and get used to low-slung jeans and quirky t-shirts instead.

🕒 *Mon–Sat, 12pm–11pm; Sun, 12pm–10.30pm; Food, Mon–Sun, 3pm–9.30pm*

White Horse

94 Brixton Hill, SW2

(020) 8678 6666

⊖ Brixton

This trendy pub-cum-club has just about got it all. There are decent snacky bar dishes (think marinated olives, wedges etc), over-the-top cocktails (so many ingredients you could hurl just reading the menu), slouchy sofas and a hip young crowd. Music is creative with your bog standard beats and breaks giving way to some interesting new stuff. And here the frantic raver feel of the Brixton of old is totally dead in the water. Raise a glass to the great god of tie-dye and give a moment's silence for the party posse.

🕒 *Mon–Wed, 5pm–12am; Thu, 2pm–1am; Fri, 2pm–3am; Sat, 12pm–3am; Sun, 12pm–10.30pm; Food, Mon–Sat, 6pm–10pm;*

BRIXTON CLUBS

The Dogstar

389 Coldharbour Lane, SW9

(0207) 7733 7515

⊖ Brixton

This cavernous barn of a place is a Brixton legend, getting a mention in The Streets' *Too Much Brandy*. For tanked-up evenings out, birthday shenanigans and even relaxed, hangover afternoons, it really can't be beaten. By night hip-hop, cheese and house DJs keep the crowd dancing, while during the day you can sink into the sofas, enjoy reasonably-priced drinks and feast on bar snacks. If you're seriously hungry, try MoCa, the Caribbean restaurant upstairs, for a serious meal.

☺ *Sun–Thu, 12pm–2am; Fri–Sat,*

Mass

St Matthews Church, Brixton Hill, SW2

(020) 7738 7875

⊖ Brixton

A Brixton institution. Mass is as much part of the local scene as Jimmy Cliff, pub-raves, boarders and jerk chicken. If you still haven't been, get yourself down the church and do penance. If you're a regular, then we know we're preaching to the converted. New management means more great nights, good vibes and the same loyal punters. We wouldn;t expect anything less. The same levels of misbehaviour are still encouraged, though. So, that'll be ten 'Hail Marys' and an 'Our Father' for the bad boys at the back...

☺ *Fri–Sat, 10pm–6am*

Fridge

Town Hall Parade, SW2

(020) 7326 5100

⊖ Brixton

Wallflowers need not apply. You're looking at club-kids on a one-way trip to self-destruction and rampant hedonism, and they'll be up 'til way past your bedtime. Yep, things get pretty crazy down The Fridge, which is the way we at Itchy like it. For those of you that didn't live it the first time round, this means a second chance to wave your hands in the air and feel like the king of the world. Nights span hard house and drum'n'bass, and the theme is always mayhem. Come on you ravers – feel the noise.

☺ *Thu, 8pm–1am; Fri–Sat, 10pm–6am*

BRIXTON RESTAURANTS

Asperanza

16a Coldharbour Lane, SE5

(020) 7738 5585

⊖ Brixton/Denmark Hill (BR)

Fetch me my velvet pantaloons and cravat! Intimate, with a thespian air, this place is great for illicit dinners or recovery lunches. Entertainment is provided by the waiters who walk the fine line between charming and 'don't give a toss about your food'. But you won't be concentrating on the grub. You'll be pointing over your shoulder, saying, 'Isn't that him from the National?'.

🕒 *Mon, closed; Tue–Fri, 12pm–3pm & 7pm–10pm; Sat, 12pm–10pm; Sun, 11am–6pm;*

🍴 *Mains, £7.95*

💰 *£8.95*

Bamboula

12 Acre Lane, SW9

(020) 7737 6633

⊖ Brixton

A trip down Brixton way just wouldn't be complete without a dose of decent Caribbean food. Here you'll find things home-cooked, fresh, tasty and served up with more charm than any sane-minded Londoner can handle. It's like walking into a different world where everything is Fanta-ad fantastic, smiling and bathed in sunshine. God knows how they manage this with just a few bits of raffia and some poster paint, but they do. Such is the spirit of Bamboula. Let it suck you in.

🕒 *Mon–Fri, 11am–11pm; Sat, 12pm–11pm*

🍴 *Bamboula flamed jerk chicken, £5*

💰 *£10.50*

Brixton Bar and Grill

15 Atlantic Road, SW9

(0207) 7737 6777

⊖ Brixton

Under the railway arches, this is a low-lit, sexy place with leather chairs, dark wood fittings and a chandelier. It delights and irritates the locals in equal numbers: some see it as the flagship of a chic new Brixton, others as a yuppie hangout. By south-of-the-river standards it's not cheap, but the luscious cocktails, tempting 'world tapas' dishes, decent DJs and super-friendly staff help justify the West End prices.

🕒 *Tue–Wed, 4.30pm–12am; Thu, 4.30pm–1am; Fri–Sat, 4.30pm–2am; Sun, 3.30pm–11pm*

🍴 *Pork loin fillet with crispy salad, £13.50*

💰 *£13*

Neon

71 Atlantic Road, SW9

(020) 7738 6576

⇌ **Brixton**

Thankfully this restaurant doesn't live up its garish name; it's much more understated with simple pasta dishes served in a cafeteria-style setting, a breezy atmosphere and the fastest service this side of Brixton High Road. We've always liked it for a quiet breather on a Sunday afternoon. Sometimes Brixtonia and it's range of loons can get too much. Try to get a seat in the window and watch the world go prancing by.

🕑 *Tue–Thu, 6pm–12am; Fri, 6pm–2am; Sat, 12pm–2am; Sun, 12pm–11pm*

🍴 *Seafood risotto, £8.95*

❷ *£12.45*

Noodle House

426 Coldharbour Lane, SW9

(020) 7274 1492

⇌ **Brixton**

Sometimes all you need is a bowl of something hot, cheap, healthy, tasty and filling. At those times you should hot-foot it to the Noodle House. There's no fuss, no fancy décor and the kind of speed-of-light service that leaves you dazed and confused; but pre-pub/deranged house party it more than fills a hole. We always wind up going for the seafood specials, but you're probably much more adventurous.

🕑 *Mon–Thu, 12pm–11.30pm; Fri–Sat, 12pm–12am; Sun, 3pm–11.30pm*

🍴 *Seafood special noodles, £4.95*

❷ *£7.95*

SW9

11 Dorrell Place, SW9

(020) 7738 3116

⇌ **Brixton**

Brixton's very own rehab clinic. Bring them a hangover of momentous proportions and let them wipe it out through the power of Bloody Mary's and breakfast goods. Brunches here are drawn out, chilled out and totally delicious. They're so good, in fact, that we've known the totally incurable to leave here with a spring in their step and plans to spend the rest of the day making stencils for the bathroom. Impressive stuff.

🕑 *Sun–Wed, 10am–11pm; Thu, 10am–12am; Fri–Sat, 10am–1am; Food, Mon–Sun, 10am–9.30pm*

🍴 *Beefburger, £7.50*

❷ *£10.50*

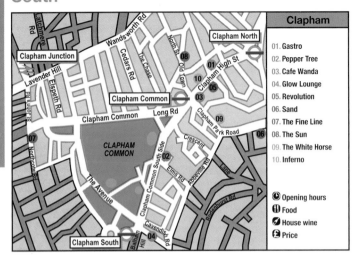

Clapham

01. Gastro
02. Pepper Tree
03. Cafe Wanda
04. Glow Lounge
05. Revolution
06. Sand
07. The Fine Line
08. The Sun
09. The White Horse
10. Inferno

🕐 Opening hours
🍴 Food
🍷 House wine
💲 Price

CLAPHAM BARS

The Fine Line

33 Northcote Road, SW11

(020) 7924 7387

🚉 Clapham Junction (BR)

Cocoon your shame in a soothing booth on those particularly painful mornings after. Here you'll find some of the best breakfast options on the Northcote Road, including a Bloody Mary that will sort you out briskly and effectively. Considering you'd have to start queuing before you started drinking the night before to have a hope of getting into some of the other breakfast hangouts around here, this is quite useful.

🕐 *Mon–Sat, 12–10pm; Sun, 11–9pm*

🍴 *Full Monty, £7.50*

💲 *£13*

Holy Drinker

59 Northcote Road, SW11

(020) 7801 0544

🚉 Clapham Junction (BR)

This long, split level room is furnished with a quirky mish-mash of furniture (burgundy flip down cinema seats, red velour chaise long, tall wooden stools) and plenty of battered pine tables to rest your (ten or so) real ales upon. Outside, there's seating should you want to have a nosy at the Battersea baby–boomers. Spirits are free–poured which is always a bonus and lights floods in through huge Artex windows. Lovely spot with more character than the All Bar One down the road... a Holy lot more in fact.

🕐 *Mon to Fri, 4.30pm–11.pm; Sat, 12pm–11pm; Sun, 10pm–10.30pm*

Matilda

74/76 Battersea Bridge Road, SW11

(020) 7228 6482

⊖ Clapham Junction (BR)

Matilda's has lovely charcuterie and cheese platters with well-sourced ingredients, great bread and an impressive wine list. A light and airy bar, there are two white rooms with well-spaced mismatched wooden tables and chairs, sofas, chandeliers and charming clutter. It boasts an open kitchen and a cute terrace for warmer weather. The crowd are of the more mature Battersea set – it's well-bred and does bread well.

⊙ *Mon–Sat, 12pm–12am;*
Sun, 12pm–11.30pm

⊕ *Chargrilled swordfish steak, £11.00*

⊘ *£11.50*

Sand

156 Clapham Park Road, SW4

(020) 7622 3022

⊖ Clapham Common/Brixton

One of the better late-drinking haunts in South London, Sand offers a touch of low-key style to SW4's 'seen it all before' types. Join them in the stone-coloured interior for cocktails, beers and shabby-chic sofas. Seating is at a premium so try and bag some early on. Otherwise, come 10pm you'll be part of the sofa stand-off – all stilted conversation and eagle eyes – rather than lounging on your chair with a view of the action.

⊙ *Mon–Sat, 5pm–2am; Sun, 5pm–1am;*
Food, Mon–Sun, 6.30pm–10.30pm

⊕ *Prawns wrapped in filo pastry, £4.95*

⊘ *£13*

Revolution

95 – 97 Clapham High Street, SW4

(020) 7720 6642

⊖ Clapham Common

There are two kinds of people: those that think this is great, and those that hate it with a passion. For some of you, it's a laid-back lounge bar playing funky vocal house and serving seventy brands of premium vodka, with just enough party poke to move aside sofas at the weekends. For others, it's just an unwelcome reminder of your misspent mid-twenties, and of that night you snogged the girl with the abscess and ended up needing to have three molars removed.

⊙ *Sun–Thu, 11.30am–12 30am; Fri–Sat,*
11.30am–2am

⊕ *BBQ chicken, £4*

⊘ *£8.95*

South

CLAPHAM PUBS

Bread & Roses
68 Clapham Manor Street, SW4
(020) 7498 1779
⊖ Clapham Common/Clapham North

Bread & Roses dishes up the beer garden of your dreams as well as an upstairs function room for events (poetry readings, comedy and the like) and plenty of liberal-minded spirit. It's owned by the Workers Beer Company and veers towards the socialist and worthy side of things. Food is hearty pub-grub and the mood is upbeat. In fact the only problem here is the small people (rug rats, not the dwarves) – they let them in till 9pm and things can reach crèche-like proportions.

Ⓒ Mon–Sat, 12pm–11pm;
Sun, 12pm–10.30pm

The Greyhound
Battersea High Street, SW11
(020) 7978 7021
⊖ Clapham Junction (BR)

Painted in warm autumnal colours with comfy seating, this intimate, sophisticated gastopub is cosy and likeable. But more than that, this Battersea pub is the place for foodies (a three–course dinner costs £28) and wine–lovers. Fancy restaurant critics have raved about the beautifully presented Modern British dishes and the extensive list of wines is excellent with prices that range from average to astronomical (there's a sommelier on hand if you need any help). For lovers of all things gastronomic The Greyhound is the absolute dog's….

Ⓒ Mon–Sat, 12pm–11pm;
Sun, 12pm–10.30pm

The Sun
47 Clapham Old Town, SW4
(020) 7622 4980
⊖ Clapham Common

In the summer this is the spot to see and be seen – the good time boys and good time girls spill out of the ample sized beer garden with their overpriced pints in their far-too-tight t-shirts. Right next to the common it's a popular spot to stop for some sun and fun, although in the winter it's really nothing but an expensive, crowded, smoky hole that's far too small and noisy to stay very long. Head to the Frog, a few doors down, for a much nicer atmosphere.

Ⓒ Mon–Sat, 11–11pm; Sun, 12–10.30pm
Ⓘ Pad Thai, £5.50
Ⓐ £11

CLAPHAM CLUBS

The Clapham Grand

21–25 St John's Hill, SW11

(0871) 474 5684

Clapham Common

To hear gems like *Brown Eyed Girl* on loop throughout the evening, come to the Clapham Grand. Listen to Toploader until your guts are ready to explode onto semi-digested drinks onto the *Saturday-Night-Fever*-inspired illuminated floor. Later in the evening, female 'dancers' appear and simultaneously suffer some kind of terrifying fit in front of a gawping, baseball-capped audience, leaving you apologising to whoever you brought here. Strictly for the masochists.

Times vary, according to club nights

Inferno's

146 Clapham High Street, SW4

(020) 7720 7633

Clapham Common

This place makes the Grand look like the classiest joint on the planet. Inferno's is pure trash and then some, but it can be a heap of fun with the right crew. Slip down a side street to find the entrance, join the assembled drunken throng, then fling your arms around to Girls Aloud and Abba until you fall over. If you're reading this now and thinking, 'No way, mate you can forget that...' we'd love to see you argue after ten pints down the High Street. Inferno's has an inbuilt magnet facility that means drunkards can't see sense.

Thu, 9pm–2am; Fri–Sat, 9pm–3am

The White House

Clapham Park Road, SW4

(020) 7498 3388

Clapham Common

If your only aim in life is to own the latest designer gear and you would easily consider cutting off your own foot if you thought it would make you more fashionable, then visit the White House. Another 'trendy' bar and restaurant for those who wish they lived in Hoxton. Do you feel a tinge of despair when you find out that your best friend has the latest mobile phone and you don't'? If you do trendy then you do the White House. If you like unpretentious food with unassuming people, then you don't.

Mon–Wed, 5.30pm–2am; Thu–Sat, 5.30pm–3am; Sun, 7pm–6am

South

CLAPHAM CAFÉS

Café Wanda

153 Clapham High Street, SW4

(020) 7738 8760

⊖ Clapham Common

A low-key caff-cum-restaurant serving up British classics alongside Polish specialities, cakes and coffees. By night it fills up with romancing couples, by day kids run riot with the waiters, while families chow down on a hearty lunch. The blinis are excellent, likewise the afore-mentioned cakes. Service is buzzy and there's outside seating for summer days.

☻ *Mon–Fri, 12pm–11pm;*
Sat–Sun, 11am–11pm

🍴 *Beef stroganoff, £9.95*

💰 *£10.50*

Glow Lounge

6 Cavendish Parade, SW4

(020) 8673 4455

⊖ Clapham South

First and foremost an Internet café, you'll want to check more than your e-mails in this place. Its comfy, squishy seating ensures a lounge-loving crowd who'd stay all day if the boutique beers and fine wines were free. The full English breakfast will sort you out on a hung-over morning, the salads, cakes and gorgeous pastries are also top-notch, and some of the best coffee in the area will give you a buzz, if the hot looking Clapham talent doesn't do it first.

☻ *Mon–Fri, 7.30am–8pm;*
Sat–Sun, 9.30am–7pm

🍴 *Full Monty, £9.95*

CLAPHAM RESTAURANTS

El Rincon Latino

148 Clapham Manor Street, SW4

(020) 7622 0599

⊖ Clapham Common

Boozy and boisterous, it's easy to forget that people actually come here for the food. But hidden behind the slurred confessions, you'll find some really rather good Spanish fare. Tapas is the popular choice and spot-on for soaking up your Rioja. The waiters here don't even bat an eyelid when you emerge from the toilets wearing someone else's clothes with a plant pot on your head.

☻ *Mon–Fri, 6.30–11.30pm; Sat, 11am–11pm;*
Sun, 11am–10.30pm

🍴 *Meatballs, £4.50*

💰 *£10.75*

Fish in a Tie

105 Falcon Road, SW11
(020) 7924 1913
🚇 Clapham Junction (BR)

Allo, allo... what is zis? 'Ave I accidentlee taken zee Euro Star from Waterloo and ended up in zee art of gay Paree? Err... no. You've just discovered this rather Moulin-Rouge-esque French restaurant in the heart of the Clapham ghetto. As Edith Piaf warbles about her pain you'll soon feel as laid-back as an Alpine farm-boy, while you guzzle deliciously cheap French cuisine. Only thing sacré bleu about this place is where it is, leave armed with a French stick and you'll make it home alive.

🕐 *Mon–Sat 12pm–3pm & 6pm–12am;*
Sun, 12pm–12am
🍴 *Warm balsamic chicken salad, £5.95*
💷 *£9.25*

Pepper Tree

19 Clapham Common Southside, SW4
(020) 7622 1758
🚇 Clapham Common

Places like this are what make London special. Places where really good food comes with a price tag from heaven, meaning you can still afford the bus to work the next day. Not only that, but the service is value for money too: the waiters here couldn't be much nicer. We absolutely love Pepper Tree with its clean, minimal décor and fuss-free Thai curries. So will you.

🕐 *Mon, 12pm–3pm & 6pm–10.30pm;*
Tue–Sat, 12pm–3pm & 6pm–11pm; Sun,
12pm–10.30pm
🍴 *Big tum prawn noodles, £5.45*
💷 *£9.50*

Gastro

67 Venn Street, SW4
(020) 7627 6222
🚇 Clapham Common

Not the kind of crappy 'gastro' pub where you pay six pounds for a baguette. It's a restaurant. A real French restaurant, which means it serves something called 'food'. The menu is terrific but the service leaves something to be desired. Lots of French waiters who can't speak English, so forget about trying to explain that your steak is overdone. These guys take a great deal of pride in ignoring their customers and looking down their nose at you like the trash that you are. We love it. Oi, Garçon... bill!

🕐 *Mon–Sun, 7am–12pm*
🍴 *£12.80 for 12 oysters*
💷 *£13*

South

BOROUGH

Baltic

74 Blackfriars Road, SE1

(020) 7928 1111

⊖ Southwark

Designed for the bleakest of Siberian mid-winter nights, Baltic's dishes will leave you with a glorious warm feeling inside. The ultra-chic bar is a setting for working through the selection of home-made flavoured vodkas. The service is painfully slow and the modernist décor leaves you with little visual interest between courses. But it is elegant, impressive and affordable.

© *Mon–Fri, 12pm–3.30pm & 6pm–11.30pm; Sat, 12pm–2.30pm & 6pm–11pm; Sun, 12pm–10.30pm*

⑪ *Platters, £10.50-£14.50*

Glas

3 Park Street, SE1

(020) 7357 6060

⊖ London Bridge

A smart restaurant near London Bridge, launched by Ann Mossenon, who foodies will know from her famous Scandelicious stall in Borough Market. Creating a smorgasbord (ouch) of a menu from prime Swedish produce, simple dishes start from only £3.95. The homemade gravadlax is top-notch, while it's worth checking/necking the range of sweet white wines. Those of you who remember the Swedish chef off the muppets would do well to leave your best impressions of the accent at home.

© *Mon–Sat, 12pm–11pm*

⑪ *Tasting dishes, £4-6*

❷ *£11.95*

Hot Stuff

19 Wilcox Road, SW8

(020) 7720 1480

⊖ Vauxhall

With more Spice than an old Geri Halliwell album, this BYO in Vauxhall offers some of the best Indian in London and comes with a satisfaction-guaranteed recommendation from the locals. Owned by the lovely Raj and family, you'll never go short on service with a smile and when you never have to pay more than £15 for three fantastic courses of authentic, delicious Indian, and you can take your own beer (next door's supply is cheap), why wouldn't you be grinning?

© *Mon–Fri, 11.30pm–9.30pm; Sat, 3pm–9.30pm; Sun, 11.30pm–9.30pm*

GREENWICH

Goddard's Pie House

45 Greenwich Church Street, SE10

(020) 8293 9313

⊖ Greenwich (DLR)

It's 1697. Sir Frances Chichester has returned from his solo circumnavigation of the globe, and is sailing up the Thames to Greenwich. On the quayside, the Queen waits to knight him with the same sword that Elizabeth I used to dub Sir Frances Drake. What actually happened was that he got there the day before, didn't tell anyone, and secretly popped into Goddard's for double pie and mash.

🕒 *Mon–Fri, 10am–6.30pm;*
Sun–Sat, 10am–7.30pm

🍴 *Pie, mash and liquor, £2*

Gipsy Moth

60 Greenwich Church St, SE10

(020) 8858 0786

⊖ Greenwich (DLR)

Ahoy me hearties! All aboard the Gipsy Moth for a yo-ho-ho and a bottle of rum. Most pubs in Greenwich are grundy affairs, catering for American tourists in day-glo shorts and Haiwaiian shirts. The Gipsy Moth has gone all out to win the yoof vote, so they've shipped in (geddit?) a stack of comfy sofas and gave the place a lick of paint. They have a decent beer garden out back and do some cracking barbecues during the summer. However, all refurbs come at a price, so expect to dig deep for your fancy Belgian beer.

🕒 *Mon–Sat, 12–11pm; Sun, 12pm–10.30pm*

South

WATERLOO

Anchor & Hope

36 The Cut, SE1

(020) 7928 9898

🚇 Waterloo

A great place to bring a few mates and stuff yourselves, though the aproned staff are more interested in keeping the whole thing moving than paying you much attention. The varied menu is chalked-up daily and to get the most out of it, share smaller dishes tapas style, or chip in together for a massive roast. Arrive early to avoid disappointment.

🕐 Mon, 5pm–11pm; Tue–Sat, 11am–11pm; Food, Mon, 6pm–10.30pm; Tue–Sat 12–2.30pm & 6–10.30pm;

🍴 Crab on toast, £6

💰 £15.00

Marie's Café

90 Lower Marsh, SE1

(020) 7928 1050

🚇 Lower Marsh

From the outside Marie's is just what you'd expect in this neck of the woods. A dingy, old fashioned greasy spoon, serving the local market. But it's a café with a difference. Being Thai-run means that as well as your usual bacon-and-egg-style fry-ups there's a smallish menu of cheap, tasty and generously portioned Thai food. Spoilt for choice. You lucky buggers.

🕐 Mon–Fri, 7am–6pm (English & Thai); 6pm–10pm (Thai food only; evenings); Sat, 7am–2pm; 5.30pm–10.30pm; Sun, closed

🍴 Between £4–£5

💰 BYO, £1 per head corkage

Meson Don Felipe

53 The Cut, SE1

(020) 7928 3237

🚇 Southwark

Deceptively small, despite its large exterior this noisy place has an authentic tapas bar atmosphere. The food is average, though portions are generous, and it's handy if you're going to the Old Vic Theatre. However, if you like to pamper your posterior, beware, the wooden seats are downright uncomfortable and almost matched in hardness by the bread rolls. Those seeking comfort and relaxation might want to look elsewhere. Look out for the flamenco guitar player perched up near the ceiling. Poor sod.

🕐 Mon–Sat, 12pm–11pm

🍴 Variety of tapas, between £4–£5

💰 £12.95

RIVERSIDE PUBS

The Dove

24 Broadway Market
020 7275 7617

Bethnal Green

Located near to the picturesque canal that runs through Broadway Market, and housing one of the finest selection of beers outside Belgium, makes this place an ideal spot to while away a lazy summer's day. The kooky approach to interior decor that teams leopard–print cushions with dark wood adds a unique touch to the place. Go wild.

Tattershall Castle

Victoria Embankment
020 7839 6548

Embankment

Not so much a riverside pub as a river-middle pub, this ex-passenger ferry moored just off the Embankment allows you to experience the river so up close and personal that every time a cargo boat goes by, you'll be holding onto your pint for dear life. Ideal for those looking for life on the ocean wave. Sea legs essential; armbands optional.

Anchor Tavern

34 Park Street
020 7407 1577

London Bridge

Those with a perverse interest in the capital's bridges will be pleased to note that you can see six of them from this pub. Tick. We'll leave you to figure out which one is most famous for being the site that Samuel Pepys watched the fire of London from. Hmmm. More recently, the pub was used to film one of the scenes from Mission Impossible.

The Gun

27 Coldharbour
020 7352 1820

North Greenwich

Nominally a gastropub, but the half of the pub lined with rows of tables covered in white linen screams restaurant at you. Stunning views across the Thames towards the Millennium Dome mean that come summer you'll end up shunning the cosy log fires for an outside seat, looking at the fattest waste of money the capital has ever seen.

IS IT A BIRD?
IS IT A PLANE?

No, it's your all-dancing,
all-singing Itchy City magazine.

The launch issue will be crash-landing near you this
spring. Containing all the usual Itchy gubbins to spice
up your life, as well as all the best in up-and-coming
music, comedy, competitions and freebie vouchers too.
Don't say we don't treat you right. To get your paws on
a copy, e-mail us at: subscriptions@itchymedia.co.uk

Itchy

West

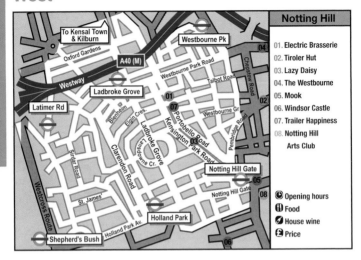

Notting Hill

01. Electric Brasserie
02. Tiroler Hut
03. Lazy Daisy
04. The Westbourne
05. Mook
06. Windsor Castle
07. Trailer Happiness
08. Notting Hill Arts Club

🕒 Opening hours
🍴 Food
🍷 House wine
💷 Price

NOTTING HILL BARS

The Lonsdale

48 Lonsdale Road, W11

(020) 7727 4080

⊖ Notting Hill Gate/Ladbroke Grove

If only places like this lost the attitude and accepted the fact that all they do is sell booze, food and somewhere to park your arse. Then you wouldn't be so disappointed having got yourself on the 'exclusive' guestlist and passed through the well-chaperoned doors. Droolingly cool, with its Barbarella-meets-Soho design, but the bevvy of tourists squatting on the velveteen poufs show just how unexceptional it is.

🕒 *Mon-Sun, 6.30pm–11.30pm*

🍴 *Fillet of Welsh beef with shallots, £10.50*

💷 *£14*

Mook

90 Notting Hill Gate, W11

(020) 7229 5396

⊖ Notting Hill Gate

On the corner of Notting Hill Gate, there's been a bit of a style revolution – now there's a surprise. What was once a dirty-carpeted, fag-burned hole is now a clean, ultra-modern bar with decent sounds and no real lighting to speak of. Unfortunately its proximity to the tube doesn't necessarily work in its favour and there is a strong ruck-sacked and kagooled contingent really digging the London vibe. However, if you can find your own space, Mook's fine for a tipple, a laugh and learning some new continental kissing techniques.

🕒 *Mon-Thu, 11am–11pm; Fri-Sat, 11am–12am; Sun, 11am–10.30pm*

Trailer Happiness

117 Portobello Road, W11

(020) 7727 2700

⊖ Notting Hill Gate

We're a bit dubious about sharing this one, as it's already getting more and more difficult to squeeze in on a weekend. But that's because once you've crept through the palm trees and sipped a £4 cocktail amongst glam West Londoners and media luvvies you actually won't hate, this Waikiki wonder will keep you coming back for more. After all, how often do you find a place that lets you escape London without hopping a plane from Heathrow?

🕒 Tue–Fri, 5–11pm; Sat, 6–11pm;
Sun, 6–10.30pm

🍸 Julio's margarita, £6.50

NOTTING HILL PUBS

Grand Union

45 Woodfield Road, W9

(020) 7286 1886

⊖ Westbourne Park

This Notting Hill boozer is still in the top ten of our 'Pubs We'd Marry (If They Were People)'. Rammed with hotties and funksters from all over the best parts of the city, with an outside bit that makes you come over all continental when it's hot, we defy you not to fall in love with it too.

🕒 Mon–Sun, 11am–11pm; Food served daily

🍴 Baked breast of chicken, £9.50

💷 £11.25

Windsor Castle

114 Campden Hill Road, W8

(020) 7243 9551

⊖ Notting Hill Gate

A comfy old slipper of a pub. It's a Dickensian haunt, with low doors in wooden panels for you to creep through. They always have a decent selection of beers and ales on tap. It has a huge (well, for London) beer garden too. Put it this way, at Christmas, when the place was bedecked with holly and candles, Team Itchy asked if we could live here.

🕒 Mon–Sat, 12pm–11pm; Sun, 12pm–10.30pm

🍴 Rosemary & chilli sausages with mash, £9

💷 £11

Due to last year's re-jigging of licensing hours, you can get a drink up to the closing times listed, but you might get some bonus drinking time too. Result! **Itchy**

West

Portobello Star

171 Portobello Road, W11

(020) 7229 8016

⊖ Notting Hill Gate/Ladbroke Grove

Patronised by people who'd touch your bum/snub you soon as look at you, this is that den of iniquity your mother warned you about. Often touted as the inspiration for The Black Cross in Martin Amis's London Fields, wander in here and you'll be met with toothless gents in rotting suits, busty ladies with lusty glances and the odd wide-eyed tourist asking where the Blue Door is. Absolute salt of the earth and perfect for those nights when you feel like getting hammered and offering someone out over a pork scratching.

🕒 *Mon–Sat, 11am–11pm; Sun, 12pm–10.30pm; Food, Sat–Sun, 11am–4pm*

Twelfth House

35 Pembridge Road, W10

(020) 7727 9620

⊖ Notting Hill Gate

If you've ever thought, 'You know what I fancy with my bottle of red tonight – my bloody horoscope read, that's what!' then you're going to think you've died and gone to heaven. For an additional £5 you can sit in this delicious cafe-restaurant-bar with candles and deep cosy seating quaffing good wine and nibbles, gazing out on Pembridge Villas while the lovely host tells you exactly why you don't like Mondays (it's something to do with Uranus).

🕒 *Tue–Sat, 9am–11pm; Sun, 9.30am–10.30pm; Food served daily*

🍴 *Greek salad, £6*

💰 *£13*

The Westbourne

101 Westbourne Villas, W2

(020) 7221 1332

⊖ Westbourne Park/Royal Oak

Now then. We're the first to admit that we used to shun this place like a hard-done-by ex. But then a mate of a mate started to fancy the barman, and so we found ourselves hanging out here and we gotta say, it sure as hell grows on you. Don't be put off by the packs of sock-less wonders or the brooding women who smoke too much and flick ash on your coat without saying sorry. Lurking among them are some really quite beautiful people and the cheese dinner is sex on a plate.

🕒 *Mon–Sun, 11am–11pm Food, Mon–Fri 12.30pm–3pm & 7pm–10.30pm; Sat–Sun, 12pm–3.30pm & 7pm–9.30pm*

NOTTING HILL CLUBS

Cherry Jam

58 Porchester Road, W2

(020) 7727 9950

⊖ Royal Oak/Bayswater

Way up there on the funkiness scale, Cherry Jam is slightly off the beaten track. From chilled early evening grooves to 'Metropolitan' and 'Urban Lounge' evenings, visitors get their money's worth of booty-shaking. Unfortunately, Saturdays can get frustratingly packed, and the occasional attendance of C-listers can take off the edge somewhat. Then again, Madonna is rumoured to have popped in.

© *Thu, 7pm–1am; Fri & Sat, 7pm–1.30am;*

Sun, 6pm–12.30am

Ⓘ *Mussels and chips, £9.95*

Notting Hill Arts Club

21 Notting Hill Gate, W11

(020) 7792 2521

⊖ Notting Hill Gate

Down in the depths of the Gate you'll find this super-trendy place, packed with a young art-funk crowd. Get down to the beats and be blown away by the massive fans on the dance floor, chill on the lazy couches or take a leaning position at the bustling bar. Wednesday offers the famous McGee & Watson Death Disco with an array of live rock bands. Latino breaks blast out on Thursday and Saturday and it gets all Hip Hoppy on Friday. Often gets absolutely packed so go early to avoid the queues.

© *Tue–Wed, 6pm–1am; Thu–Fri, 6pm–2am;*

Sat, 4pm–2am; Sun, 4pm–12.30am

Woody's

41–43 Woodfield Road, W9

(020) 7266 3030

⊖ Westbourne Park

Even though Itchy hates this place with a passion as yet unknown to modern man, we have to admit that Thursdays have become a little less skin-crawling. They have live performances from bands and MCs, which almost make up for the endless groping and general all-round poor behaviour of the regular clientele. Oddly enough, this crew includes the likes of Kate Moss (when she's actually in the country). The other nights are business as usual: over-priced, over-familiar and over-rated. *Shudder*.

© *Thu, 9pm–3am; Fri, 9pm–3am; Sat,*

9pm–3am; Sun, 8pm–1am

West

NOTTING HILL CAFÉS

Lazy Daisy

59a Portobello Road, W11

(020) 7221 8416

⊖ Notting Hill Gate

This cafe is smack-bang in the middle of nappy valley, but use that as an excuse to indulge your inner child. Anyone for fishfingers and baked beans? It's tucked away off the main drag, so you can avoid the tourists and rest a while before sharpening your elbows to fight for cashmere at the market under the Westway. Make sure you're on a sugar high before you get back out there. Seconds out, round two...

☻ *Mon–Sat, 9am–5pm; Sun, 12–2.30pm*

🍽 *Quiche and chips, £5*

Notting Hill Brasserie

92 Kensington Park Road, W11

(020) 7229 4481

⊖ Notting Hill Gate

For those outside of London the words 'Notting Hill' tend to be associated with a saccharine Hollywoood blockbuster; which would normally be inappropriate for a high-end restaurant. But not in this case, because the Notting Hill Brasserie is tinseltown all over: celebs earnestly deliver their dialogue to each other in an atmospherically lit setting. This place has one of the tastiest menus that the capital has to offer.

☻ *Mon–Sat, 12pm–3pm & 7pm–11pm; Sun, 12pm–3pm*

🍽 *Roast loin of venison with cabbage, £23.50*

💰 *£15*

NOTTING HILL RESTAURANTS

Electric Brasserie

191 Portobello Road, W11

(020) 7908 9696

⊖ Notting Hill Gate/Ladbroke Grove

Ignore the posh, poncey bastards gathered around the bar like over-coiffed seals and book yourself a nice'n'cosy booth at the back for proper luxury. A perfect round off to a night at the sumptuous cinema next door, which has its own bar and tubs of comfort food. This place is quintessential Notting Hill.

☻ *Mon–Thu, 8am–12am; Fri–Sat, 8am–2am; Sun, 8am–12am*

🍽 *Duck cottage pie, £12*

💰 *£12.50*

Ripe Tomato

7 All Saints Road, W11

(020) 7565 0525

⊖ Notting Hill Gate

This family-run Italian is quite a walk from the tube, but you'll work up your appetite on the way there. And you'll be glad you did. It's small, cozy and candlelit – you can almost imagine lady and the tramp doing the old spaghetti trick in a quiet corner. Awwww. The lasagne is to die for and the pizzas are infinitely better than the sorry Pizza Express excuses round the corner. Authentic Italian at affordable prices. If you're trying to impress a laydee, bring her here for a spot of genuine amore.

☻ *Mon–Sat, 7pm–11.15pm; Sun, 6.30pm–10.30pm*

Shish

71–75 Bishops Bridge Road, W2

(020) 7229 7300

⊖ Bayswater/Royal Oak

The moon on a stick? Not quite, but you will get just about everything else on a stick here. The chaps at Shish have decided that sticking something on a skewer is the best way to cook it. So that's what they do. Dishes are inspired by ingredients found along the length of the Silk Road, so you'll find yourself enjoying flavours from Italy to Japan, and everything in between. Whatever you order you'll find it's been lovingly spiked and cooked to perfection.

⏰ *Mon–Fri, 11am–12am; Sat, 10.30am–12am; Sun, 10.30am–11pm*

🍴 *Persian kofta, £5.75*

Tiroler Hut

27 Westbourne Grove, W2

(020) 7727 3981

⊖ Bayswater/Royal Oak

Dinner, the Austrian way. Make yourself comfy, then polish off a huge plate of sausage and sauerkraut. Wash it all down with bierstein after bierstein of strong lager. While you do this, you will be encouraged to sing waltzers by a lederhosen-clad chap called Josef who plays an accordion in a little shed in the restaurant. If you're still conscious by the time dessert comes, he'll see him leave the shed and play any tune you request on his cowbells. Better start learning the words to *Edelweiss*....

⏰ *Tue–Sat, 6.30pm–1am; Sun, 6.30pm–11pm*

🍴 *Bratwurst with sauerkraut, £9.70*

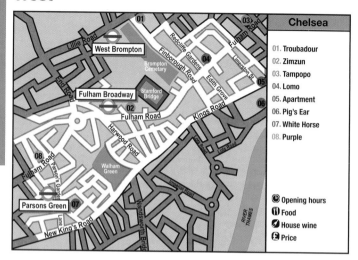

Chelsea

01. Troubadour
02. Zimzun
03. Tampopo
04. Lomo
05. Apartment
06. Pig's Ear
07. White Horse
08. Purple

⊘ Opening hours
⑪ Food
⊘ House wine
⊟ Price

CHELSEA BARS

Apartment 195

195 King's Road, SW3

(0871) 223 1092

⊖ Sloane Square

Carlsberg don't do cocktail bars, but if they did... Well, you know the strap-line. Step into a room of softly lit damson walls and chocolate brown sofas, restrained elegance and a seriously top-notch cocktail list. This bar appeared in your favourite dreams long before you knew it existed. Don't be put off by the anonymous front door and intercom system, it just adds to the cool. But it does get busy on weekends so you must remember to call ahead and put yourself on the guest list to ensure entry.

⊘ Mon–Sat, 4–11pm; Mon–Sat, 4–10 30pm

Lomo

222 Fulham Road, SW10

(020) 7349 8848

⊖ South Kensington

The perfect place to drown your sorrows when it hits you that you'll never be able to afford a pad in SW10. Join staff from the nearby hospital (they've all realised it too) for value good-vaule tapas. You'll soon come up with a list of reasons why you hate posh people. After a few glasses of Sangria things start looking up: it's all optimistic banter and flirting in this modern but comfortable restaurant/bar.

⊘ Mon–Fri, 5pm–11.30pm; Sat–Sun, 12pm–11.30pm; Sun, 5pm–11pm; Food, Mon–Sat 5pm–11pm; Sun, 5pm–11pm

⑪ Rocket and manchego salad, £4.95

⊟ £10.95

CHELSEA PUBS

Atlas

16 Seagrave Road, SW6

(020) 7385 9129

⊖ West Brompton

We're not sure if Mama would approve of the rowdy boozer environment but she'd definitely approve of the food. Atlas dishes up Med style mains at not-bad-at-all prices – great for those nights when you'd rather eat your own elbows than cook. Boozers will be equally happy; this is a real drinkers' pub. It's of the wooden boards, blackboard menu, loud acoustics ilk and there's loads of wine for the ladies. Haven't we come a long way since All Bar One?

🕗 *Mon–Sat, 12pm–11pm;*

Sun, 12pm–10.30pm;

The Builder's Arms

13 Britten Street, SW3

(020) 7349 9040

⊖ Sloane Square

Pleasantly cavernous interior. Check. Moody black-and-white photographs. Check. Cast-iron chandelier and a dishevelled bookcase with copy of Moby Dick. Check. The arrival of a real builder would have the regulars reaching instinctively for their Lulu Guinness pearl pouch bags. Full of fey Etonians smoking cigarettes with their thumbs and forefingers.

🕗 *Mon–Sat, 11am–11pm; Sun, 12pm–10pm;*

🍴 *Pan-fried duck with cabbage, £12.50*

🥂 *£11.90*

The Farm

18 Farm Lane, SW6

(020) 7381 3331

⊖ Fulham Broadway

Yet another fancy gastro pub for Fulham's wealthy and fabulous to flash their black Amex cards in. Get your ass down there and tuck into some God-like gastro grub. A near-as-damn-it perfect local in which to down a few pints, banter with your workmates or romance your latest conquest with low-key aplomb. NB They don't take cash. Yep that's right. No cash. Cash, darlings, is just sooo last year.

🕗 *Mon–Sat, 12pm–11pm; Sun, 12pm–10.30pm*

🍴 *Cornish mussels, £12.50*

🥂 *£12.95*

Due to last year's re-jigging of licensing hours, you can get a drink up to the closing times listed, but you might get some bonus drinking time too. Result! **Itchy**

West

The Pig's Ear

35 Old Church Street, SW3

(020) 7352 2908

⊖ Fulham Broadway

This gastropub in Chelsea really does offer you a pig's ear to chew on (for a quid) although there are plenty of other dishes on the seasonal menu if that doesn't appeal. Crammed full with Tarquins, Pereguins and other fancifully named visitors, there really isn't that much space in this dark green room, what with the massive central bar eating up most of it. But this high-vaulted room is nicely done out with simple but bold furnishings – love the massive mirrors. And if it's good enough for recent diner Prince William, it's good enough for us.

◉ *Mon–Sat, 12–11pm; Mon–Sat, 12–10 30pm*

The Trafalgar

200 King's Road, SW3

(020) 7349 1831

⊖ South Kensington/Sloane Square

This large open space has the bar slap-bang in the middle (so all seating is equal distance from the booze, brilliant) and a pool table in the corner. Most of the seating is made up of comfy sofas and the crowd are made up of late twenty/early thirty-something sloanies. Well, what did you expect? Food is overpriced and, in all honesty, not very good. But it's a nice spot for a quick drink (at a much more sensibly priced £4.25 for a large glass of red) after shopping along King's Road, and it's also ideal for celeb-spotting.

◉ *Mon–Sat, 12–11pm; Mon–Sat, 12–10 30pm*

The White Horse

1–3 Parsons Green, SW6

(020) 7736 2115

⊖ Parsons Green

Sloane centralis – we've always treasured a particular photo we took of this place for the sheer comedy of the outfits on show. We're talking wall-to-wall chinos, posh shirts with shorts; the whole smart-casual shebang. Good job then that this is such a good pub. If it based its business plan on the punters dress sense it'd have been dead in the water aeons ago. Enjoy proper ales, wines galore and food so beautifully prepared you'll want to snog the chef's feet in admiration.

◉ *Mon–Sat, 11am–11pm; Sun, 11am–10.30pm; Food, Mon–Fri, 12pm–3pm & 6–10.30pm; Sat–Sun, 12pm–10pm*

CHELSEA CLUBS

606 Club

90 Lots Road, SW10
(020) 7352 5953
⊖ Fulham Broadway

This cosy little Chelsea jazz club has been packing in the punters since the 80s, and is now known by many jazz aficionados as the best jazz club in Europe. Not the kind of place to head to if you're after a night on the lash, as the licence only allows them to serve alcohol with meals. They're also a bit picky about serving a 'substantial meal' to warrant booze, so be prepared. If you're an aficionado of trumpet noodling, this is the place for you.

◉ *Mon–Wed, 7.30pm–1am; Thu–Sat, 8pm–1.30am; Sun, 8pm–12am*

Purple

Chelsea Village, Stamford Bridge, SW6
(020) 7565 1445
⊖ Fulham Broadway

This is where Fulham's flash daddies' girls come in their university holidays. For some of you, this is all we need to say on the matter. For the rest of you, you might want to know that it's poncey, tacky and incredibly expensive. If you can't manage to fake some decent prospects, an aristocratic breeding, or failing that an in-depth and sensitive appreciation of India's spiritualism, you'll never manage to cop off. Mind you, it's another royal haunt, so it may be well worth sacrificing your blue-collar principles for the evening.

◉ *Mon–Thu, 9pm–1am; Fri–Sat, 9pm–2am*

West

CHELSEA CAFÉS

Mona Lisa Café

417 Kings Road, SW10

(020) 7376 5447

⊖ Sloane Square

Appropriately enough for a place named after a work of art, the meals here are lovingly crafted little works of gastronomic joy. The Eclectic East European/Italian dishes are served up along with a friendly family atmosphere and low-key buzz. Flashy this place may not be, but fortunately the food and wine does the real talking.

⊗ *Mon–Sat 6.30am–11pm;*
Sun, 8.30am–5.30pm
⊕ *Chicken spaghetti bolognaise, £5.70*
⊘ *£8.50*

Troubadour

265 Old Brompton Road. SW5

(020) 7370 1434

⊖ West Brompton

Still riding the wave of hip, arty bohemia that saw Bob Dylan and co play here back in the day, Troubadour is a bar, cafe, restaurant and arts venue in one. In fact you could pretty much live here if only they'd put a futon in a back room. Stagger in for an early breakfast and stay put for morning coffee and a scan of the papers. Dinner is buzzy, then it's cocktails, red wine and meaningful poetry/music/comedy/theatre (delete as applicable) 'til closing. A truly fabulous place to just be.

⊗ *Mon–Sun, 9am–12am*
⊕ *The Troubadour omelette, £6.95*
⊘ *£10.95*

CHELSEA RESTAURANTS

La Perla

803 Fulham Road, SW6

(020) 7471 4895

⊖ Parsons Green

A rowdy restaurant/bar that dishes up slammers, beers and Margaritas at a closing-down-sale pace. The music gets louder as the night progresses and there's always some pissed girl in the corner reckoning she's shit-hot at flamenco. She's not, but bless her for trying. Feeling peckish? A world of nachos awaits. Come Friday night this place is hedonism in a shot glass.

⊗ *Mon–Fri, 5pm–11pm; Sat,*
12pm–11pm; Sun, 12pm–10.30pm
⊕ *Barbecue spare ribs, £10.95*
⊘ *£10.50*

Olé

Broadway Chambers, Fulham Broadway, SW6

(020) 7610 2010

⊖ **Fulham Broadway**

A million miles away from your average tapas joint with a fresh, airy space and food as good as you'd find in Barcelona. Come with a crowd so you can order loads and share – dishes start at around £2 and peak at £6 so there's no need to skimp. The prawns and tortilla are spot-on washed down with a decent bottle of wine. The mood is more refined than your usual sangria and microwaved-squid-type affair, which will either put you off or have you saving the number into your mobile.

🕓 *Mon–Sat, 12pm–3pm & 5pm–11pm*

🍴 *Tapas from £2–£6*

💷 *£11*

ZimZun

Fulham Broadway Retail Centre, SW6

(020) 7385 4555

⊖ **Fulham Broadway**

Fabulously fusing Chinese, Japanese and Thai foods all for a price which doesn't make you feel like you could have flown to the Orient and cooked for yourself, you'll be glad you found ZimZun. For £20–£25 you can get a three-course meal with a glass of wine. The smiling staff, great location, posh, floating flowers and light dressings that hang ceremoniously from the ceiling like water droplets off a pagoda all make this place sparkle.

🕓 *Sun–Mon, 12–10pm; Tue–Thu, 12–10.30pm; Fri–Sat, 12–11pm*

🍴 *Coconut mange tout, £5.55*

💷 *£14.50*

Tampopo

140 Fulham Road, SW10

(020) 7370 5355

⊖ **South Kensington**

Minimalist, informal and communal dining brings itself to Fulham Road in the form of Eastern wonder Tampopo. The menu works on a street food concept. Set up by two chaps who wanted to bring their travelling experiences to the masses after university, the London branch is their fourth venture. Rice and noodles are in abundance and the handy open kitchen means you can wave goodbye to the days of gluey rice and nick expert cooking tips.

🕓 *Mon–Thu, 12pm–11pm; Fri & Sat, 12pm–11.30pm; Sun, 12pm–10pm*

🍴 *Chicken mee goring, £7.95*

💷 *£11.95*

West

QUEEN'S PARK

Curry Nights

58 Chamberlayne Road, NW10

(020) 8964 5725

↔ Queen's Park/Kensal Green

Itchy has misbehaved in here more times than we care to remember and they still seem to treat us like minor royalty. (We must have done something worthy in a past life.) Duck past the fake fire in the window to an absolute curry haven. You've got to love somewhere that finishes up every meal with a rose, free liqueur and chocolate for 'the laydees'. Admittedly, the boys in your gang will be less than impressed, Give 'em a break. Let them have a complimentary mint as you leave.

⊙ *Mon–Sun, 12pm–2pm & 6pm–12am*

Paradise by way of Kensal Green

19 Kilburn Lane, W10

(020) 8969 0098

↔ Kensal Green

A veritable oasis in the midst of north London nuttiness. Picture the scene. You've been tramping around Portobello all day and you need somewhere to rest your toes. Just pull up an armchair, get a bottle of wine and relax reading one of the books from the faux library décor. You might as well be in your living room it's so comfy. Also, for the BB aficionados among you, this is Dermot O'Leary's local. With smartly chosen tunes at the weekend, a tasty if expensive menu and a room to hire out for parties, the good times are definitely rolling in Kensal Green.

⊙ *Mon–Sat, 12pm–11pm; Sun, 12pm–10.30pm*

William IV

786 Harrow Road, NW10

(020) 8969 5944

↔ Kensal Green

One of the best gastro-pubs in London (stop yawning – it really is superb), the WIV doubles up as a great location for grabbing a roast and a few pints with your mates of a Sunday, and it's also a particularly fertile place to pull on a Friday or Saturday night. With good tunes, booze and company it don't get a lot better this close to Notting Hill. The fact that it's open until late at the weekend makes it a whole lot sweeter.

⊙ *Mon–Thu, 12pm–11pm; Fri–Sat, 12pm–1am; Sun, 12pm–10.30pm*

⑪ *Tapas about £6*

❷ *£12.50*

LITTLE VENICE

Bridge House Pub and Canal Café Theatre

Delamere Terrace, W2

(0871) 332 2701

⊖ Warwick Avenue

In keeping with the latest craze for all things vaudevillian, Bridge House's velvet–draped, gothic makeover won't disappoint either the crossword–solving Sunday drinkers or those after a livelier pint. While sampling its enviable selection of booze–you can listen to unimposing eclectic DJ sets, or pick up a board game from the bar. In the summer, watch the narrowboats slide by on Regents canal while chomping on a fishfinger buttie. Heaven.

Ⓒ *Mon–Sat, 12pm–11pm; Sun, 12pm–10.30pm*

Waterway

54–56 Formosa Street, W9

(020) 7266 3557

⊖ Warwick Avenue

Paddington Basin and its environs have had a bit of work done recently and it's actually a lovely walk up from Little Venice along the canal. See the wildlife or, alternatively, see the Waterway – a canal-side gastro-pub with a huge terrace, great food and good choons. If the sun is shining, sit outside and watch the barges go by. If it's pissing down, snuggle down on one of the leather sofas inside and watch the ducks do their thang.

Ⓒ *Mon–Sat, 12pm–11pm; Sun, 12pm–10.30pm; Food, Mon–Sun, 12.30pm–4pm & 6.30pm–10.30pm*

Ⓘ *Grilled baby squid, £7.50*

Ⓐ *£12.50*

Prince Alfred

5 Formosa Street, W9

(020) 7286 3287

⊖ Warwick Avenue

A classy haunt for the Little Venice locals, this outstanding Victorian pub has been lovingly refurbished. It's full of original features, like etchings, snob screens and funny doors at hip height (something to do with cleaners we heard) and, more importantly, has a brilliant selection of beers. If you're into intricate tiling, ornate ceilings and cosy snugs (available for hire), this is the place for you. The Formosa dining room is attached to the pub and serves up some of the finest nosh in town. We ain't gonna pretend it's cheap, but neither are you.

Ⓒ *Mon–Sat, 11am–11pm; Sun, 12pm–10.30pm*

West

SHEPHERD'S BUSH

The Anglesea Arms

35 Wingate Road, W6

(020) 8749 1291

⊖ Ravenscourt Park

In an age where rustic irreverent styling has monopolised 'cool' boozer décor it is refreshing to find a place which ticks all the boxes but goes so much further. Details count and the open fire and clock stopped at 10.40pm (symbolic perhaps?) merely add to the fantastic food, tasty drinks and a convivial atmosphere for vintage conversation. Pubbing at its very best.

🍺 *Mon–Sat, 12pm–11pm; Sun, 12pm–10.30pm*

🍴 *Duck & fois gras terrine, £7.20*

💲 *£11*

Defectors Weld

170 Uxbridge Road, W12

(020) 8749 0008

⊖ Shepherd's Bush

It's difficult to eat a steak sandwich in front of someone you hardly know, especially when the onions are spilling out the sides and the ketchup's oozing onto your fingers, but it's just too good to stop. The chips here are also perfect. This one's popular with BBC staff who work just around the corner and gather nightly to huddle and mutter round the fire. It's also a great stop for tanyone going to a gig at the Empire. Relax in a huge leather sofa with a Leffe and watch the world go by.

🍺 *Mon–Thu, 12–11pm; Fri–Sat, 12pm–12am; Sun, 12–10.30pm*

The Ginglik

1 Shepherd Bush, W12

(020) 8749 2310

⊖ Shepherd's Bush

The last place you'd expect to find such an oasis of cool is in the arse end of Shepherd's Bush, especially when this bar/club had a past life as an underground public toilet. The Ginglik is a whirlwind of bohemian expression, with comedy, film and music nights, to name just a few. Every evening is different, yet they all share the same cracking formula – to the delight of the chilled-out, super hip clientele. This is the only toilet in London you'd be proud to hang around on a Saturday night.

🍺 *Sun–Wed, 7pm–12am; Thu–Sat, 7pm–1am*

🍴 *Burger, £6.75*

💲 *£11*

KEBAB SHOPS

DRUNK YOU MAY BE, BUT THAT DOESN'T MEAN YOU HAVE TO EAT SOMETHING THAT RESEMBLES SHOE LEATHER. TASTY KEBAB SHOPS AHOY....

Efes

80 Great Titchfield Street, W1

020 7636 1953

 Oxford Circus

Favourite kebab haunt of a fair few celebs, judging by the photos lining the walls. It's cheap, it's tasty and it's about the tastiest Turkish meal you're going to get round these parts. For those of you who don't have the time to settle down and take in the cosy atmosphere of the dimly–lit interior, they do a takeaway service too.

Woody's

1 Camden Road, NW1

020 7485 7774

Camden Town

Ignore the terrible 1980s pine cabin–style decor, and head on in. It's this or the minced selection of grislte that normally passes for a takeaway in Camden Town. In the short time since its opening, Woody's tasty fare has redefined NW1's afterhours nosh. The waiters wear natty (clean) waistcoats, which can only be a good thing.

Kebab Kid

90 New King's Road, SW6

020 7731 0427

Fulham Broadway

Popular with Fulham's monied-up residents, this place serves some of the best quality meat you'll find in a kebab haunt. The size of the portions alone makes this place worth a visit, so long as you can put up with all the mockney management consultants comparing business cards over a shwarma. 'Rah, rah, rah...'

Mangal Ocakbasi

10 Arcola Street, E8

020 7275 8981

Highbury and Islington

The less than salubrious environs of Dalston might not offer the biggest draws in the world, but if you're after a kebab, this is the best place to head. Many Londoners list this authentic Turkish venue and its tasty selection of dips as their favourite venue for a spot of shish indulgence. Just make sure you leave the engine running and the doors open, eh?

Gay

Gay

GAY BARS

Candy Bar

4 Carlisle Street, W1
(020) 7494 4041
⊖ Tottenham Court Road

Forget the Cheers Bar, this is the place where everyone knows your name; not least because you probably went home with them sometime last year. At the weekends it's packed to the hilt with ladies looking for a slice of the action at the popular pole-dancing nights. A visit to the Candy Bar is a must for any new girl on Sapphic street. If you like R'n'B tunes and Alex Parks/BB Kitten look-alikes, this is the place for you.

🟢 *Mon–Thu, 5pm–11.30pm; Fri–Sat, 5pm–2am; Sun, 5pm–10.30pm*

Duckie at the Vauxhall Tavern

372 Kennington Lane, SE11
(020) 7737 4043
⊖ Vauxhall

Camper than camp and not a little strange. Set in deepest sarf London, at the Vauxhall Tavern, Duckie is a club for those who like their nights cheesy and experimental. Offering up bizarre cabaret (think videos of women giving birth and people vomiting), it may not be everyone's cup of tea. However, the music is rocky/kitsch, and it makes a change from the unrelenting commercialism of G.A.Y. Go with an open mind and enjoy the fairy cakes cooked by hostess with the mostess, Amy Lame. (She's the one who starred in ITV's *Celebrity Fit Club*.) Bravo!

🟢 *Sat, 9pm–2am*

First Out

52 Street Giles High Street, WC2

(020) 7240 8042

⊖ Tottenham Court Road

First Out should be the first port of call for scene newbies. Relaxed, central and reasonably priced, it attracts a diverse crowd of gay boys and girls. It's spot-on for Sunday brunch, lunch and after-work catch-ups with friends. Not to be missed is Girl Friday, when the downstairs bar pulls in a fit young crowd and funky DJ. Whether you're here for the cheap cocktails or just a comforting pot of rosie lee, you'll soon be feeling right at home.

🕒 *Mon-Sat, 10am–11pm; Sun, 11am–10.30pm*

🍴 *Spinach and mushroom lasagne, £4.95*

💷 *£12*

G-A-Y (Bar)

30 Old Compton Street, W1

(020) 7494 2756

⊖ Leicester Square/Tottenham Court Road

G-A-Y has to be experienced – it's something of a rites of passage. Populated by people who could be characters in a Pulp song, the G-A-Y phenomenon attracts many a suburban scene queen. Situated at the never changing Astoria, it's the best place in town to get drunk on alcopops, watch the Cheeky Girls lip-synch and get your hands on an easy snog. Also, try the G-A-Y bar in Old Compton Street – it has regular drinks promotions and a lesbian bar down-stairs called 'Girls Go Down'. Classy.

🕒 *Mon-Sat, 12pm–12am;*

Sun, 12pm–10.30pm

Friendly Society

The Basement (entrance in Tisbury Court),

79 Wardour Street, W1

(020) 7434 3805

⊖ Tottenham Court Road/Leicester Square

It may come as a surprise, but The Friendly Society isn't a building society or a cult; instead, it is a veritable cornucopia of style, with a sprinkling of quirkiness. It manages to balance shagging Barbies and Babycham wallpaper with luxurious lounge music. This place is cool with a small, relaxed 'c' – no Soho snobs allowed. Ideal for pre-club drinks or midweek people watching with a DJ most evenings and a 'fairy room' that has to be seen to be believed.

🕒 *Mon-Fri, 4pm–11pm; Sat, 2pm–11pm;*

Sun, 2pm–10.30pm

Gay

Southopia

146–148 Newington Butts, SE11

(020) 7735 5306

⊖ Kennington

It's a universal truth that whilst there are many lesbians in South London, there are very few lesbian bars. Southopia plugs the gap and attracts women from all over the capital. There's top-notch food, open fires in winter and Egyptian maidens to fan you Pharaoh stylee in the summer. Yep, Southopia is the jewel of the Elephant and Castle. Don't miss the sarcophagus in the toilets and the free manicures.

☻ Mon–Thu, 5pm–10.30pm; Fri–Sat, 5pm–11pm; Sun, 12pm–10.30pm; Food, Mon–Sat, 5pm–10pm; Sun, 12pm–4pm & 6pm–9pm

⑪ Sunday roast, £6.95

❷ £10.50

GAY CLUBS

G-A-Y

London Astoria, 157 Charing Cross Road, WC2

G-A-Y Bar, 30 Old Compton Street, W1

(020) 7734 6963

⊖ Tottenham Court Road

G-A-Y is like the Vicky Pollard of the gay scene: it knows what it is and it has no shame. Every week, the campest bandwagon in town churns out performances from the stars of pop: one night you could see Girls Aloud wooing the crowds, another night it might be Mel C trying to convince all and sundry that she's a rock star. If you are a dedicated follower of cheese anthems, there's simply nowhere else to go on a Saturday night.

☻ Mon, Thu, Fri & Sat, 10.30pm–4am

Star At Night

22 Great Chapel Street

(020) 7434 3749

⊖ Tottenham Court Road/Oxford Street

There is no doubt about it, The Star at Night is a shiny delight. By day, you'll find a fairly straight crowd but by night things get seriously cosy. With its chilled atmosphere, candlelit tables and sophisticated female crowd, this is spot-on first date territory. If you're after a bit of privacy, there's a cavernous basement with gingham tablecloths. If you're feeling adventurous and are willing to make a complete fool of yourself, get stuck into the cocktails and shots. Itchy tried the Absinthe shooters with memorable (read: disastrous) results.

☻ Tue–Sat, 6pm–12am

Ghetto

Falconberg Court, W1

07956 549246

⊖ Tottenham Court Road

Self-consciously anti-Soho, The Ghetto offers a seven-day a week, freaky unique clubbing experience. With popular nights such as 'Nag, Nag, Nag' (Wednesdays), 'Don't Call Me Babe' (Tuesdays) and old favourites like 'Wig Out' (Thursdays), The Ghetto attracts a diverse crowd. Loved by the (now-defunct) Face magazine and Dazed and Confused, it attracts stars like Boy George, Siobhan Fahey and Yoko Ono for PA spots. If you like your nights out cutting-edge, this is the place to get down with the fashionistas.

☻ Mon–Sat, 10.30pm–3am; Sun, 10pm–3am

Gay

Heaven

The Arches, Villiers St, WC2
(020) 7930 2020
⊖ Embankment/Charing Cross

With a bevvy of beefcake beauties dancing to disco beats, Heaven is the club of choice for many a scene queen. Hidden away underneath Charing Cross station, and covering three floors, there's a wonderfully decadent mixture of house, techno and a sprinkling of R'n'B. Not surprising then that it's been keeping the kids happy for donkey's years. Rock up for go-go dancers, laser shows and a whole world of cruising action. Ooooh, Heaven really is a place on earth. Eyes peeled for Graham Norton.

◉ Mon–Wed, 10pm–4am; Sat, 10pm–4am

Popstarz

The Scala, 275 Pentonville Road. N1
(020) 7833 2022
⊖ King's Cross

Every Friday the indie kids come out to play at Popstarz. There are drinks promos galore, scruffy kids and an upbeat studenty feel. Shake your thing to Britpop classics and make like you're 18 all over again. There's also the cheese-fest to beat all cheese-fests in the 80s disco room for those who need a break from the sound of guitars. Leave the trade at home as there's plenty of zhoosh in here to keep you happy for the week ahead. Celeb-spotters might be lucky enough to bump into a certain bald *Little Britain* star. 'Yeah but no, but, yeah'.

◉ Fri, 10pm–5am

Too 2 Much

11 Walkers Court, W1
(020) 7734 0377
⊖ Piccadilly Circus

A relatively recent addition to the Soho club scene, this venue has knocked the Raymond Revue Bar right off its place on top of the seedy perch. Specialising in queer cabaret and excessive theatrics it's a sight to behold for anyone needing an urgent injection of glitz. Essentially, it's a tongue-in-cheek celebration of all things glam, brash and tacky, with a spot of pole dancing thrown in for good measure. If that's good enough for Sir Elton's stag night, it's good enough for you.

◉ 10pm–late

LISTEN UP
OMI PALONES!

THOSE OF YOU OUT CHARPERING FOR A DOLLY DISH WITH A NICE BASKET MIGHT WANT TO TAKE NOTE OF AN IMMINENT LINGUISTIC REVIVAL ON THE UK GAY SCENE.

Polari, the secret language used by London's 1960s gay community to communicate in public without fear of the law, has long been as dead as a dodo's cassette collection.

But the pink parlance is starting to come back out of the closet. What with a re-invigorated Morrissey being a self-confessed polari user, as well as usage of polari becoming almost compulsory amongst staff at popular London kitsch cabaret venue Madame JoJo's, it looks like pretty soon anyone who's anyone will need to know their fantabuloso lingo.

I'M BONAR FOR THAT OMI PALONE

'What a cod meese omi'
– 'What a vile ugly man'

'Vada the colour of his eyes'
- 'Check out the size of his penis'

'Vada the poloni with the matini'
- 'Look, he's gay'

'I'm bonar for that ome palone'
- 'I'm attracted to that man'

'Nice basket'
- 'Nice trouser bulge'

'You're joshed up'
– 'You're looking your best'

'Aunt Nell!'
– 'Listen to me!'

'Vada the cod zhoosh on that ome palone'
– 'Look at the awful clothes on that man'

'Nanti vogue near me'
– 'Don't light that cigarette near me'

'Let's blag some dishes'
– 'Let's pick up some good-looking guys'

'There's nix mungarlee here'
– 'There's nothing to eat here'

Shop

Shop

AREAS

Bond Street/Mayfair
⊖ Bond Street/Green Park

Fancy experiencing a day in the life of Madame Beckham? Get your best frock on and have a stroll down Bond Street. Don't miss South Molton Street, off Bond Street for shoes galore.

Covent Garden
⊖ Covent Garden/Leicester Square

Get away from the fake statues (do they really stand there all day?) and you'll arrive at a great shopping zone. If you skateboard, snowboard, or like to think that one day you might get off your arse and jump out of a plane, then head to Neal Street to get the togs.

High Street Kensington
⊖ High Street Kensington

Rich kids blowing daddy's cash and a wash of pink pashminas. Worth a look for Urban Outfitters – though there is one in Covent Garden now – and a roll call of your usual high street stuff. It's often a bit quieter than Oxford Street on a Saturday, if you need to do a weekend swoop.

Kingly Court/Carnaby Street
⊖ Oxford Circus/Piccadilly Circus

After you've taken the predictable trip down Carnaby Street, drop into spanking-new Kingly Court for a gander. You'll find several levels, filled with quirky boutiques and trendier high-street shops, all overlooking a chilled little courtyard with a café. Aaaaaah.

Knightsbridge
⊖ Knightsbridge

Home to Harrods, Harvey Nic's and Sloane Street, Knightsbridge is filled with highlighted blondes carrying rat-cum-dogs in their sequinned handbags. This is window-shopping territory for most of us, but it's still well worth a gander (if only to see how the other half live).

Oxford Street/Regent Street
⊖ Oxford Circus/Piccadilly Circus

Manic tourists, worn-out faces and every high-street shop going. TopShop and its haven of infinite fashion possibility means that there'll always be a reason to get off the bus at Oxford Circus, but for a more relaxed shopping trip, you'll need to look further afield.

MARKETS

Portobello Market

Portobello Road, W10

⊖Notting Hill Gate

Despite the tourists, Portobello manages to retain its retro chic. The Notting Hill end is all antiques, but you can still find great thrifty togs under the Westway.

Fri–Sat, 7am-7pm

Spitalfields Market

Commercial Street, E1

⊖Liverpool Street

The perfect starting point for exploring the boho East End, although most of the clothes, art and knick knacks will cost you a pretty penny.

Sun, 10am–5pm

Camden Market

Camden High Street, NW1

⊖Camden Town

Full of 15-year-olds, but Camden Market is still swinging. Packed with everything from antique rugs to herbal highs. Very mixed quality; still some bargains though.

Sat–Sun, 9am–5.30pm

Borough Market

Borough High Street, SE1

⊖London Bridge

The finest farmer's market around. Grab some outstanding picnic grub, or just peruse the produce like a gastro connoisseur. Pigs trotters with quail livers, anyone?

Fri, 9am–6pm; Sat, 9am–4pm

Shop

DEPARTMENT STORES

Harrods

87–135 Brompton Road, SW1

(020) 7730 1234

🚇 Knightsbridge

Queue in the morning for Krispy Kreme donuts, but dress nice for the door code.

🕐 *Mon–Sat, 10am–7pm; Sun, closed*

Harvey Nichols

109–125 Knightsbrid, SW1

(020) 7235 5000

🚇 Knightsbridge

Harvey Nichols is Mecca for designer junkies. Live the dream with a glass of champagne on the fifth floor.

🕐 *Mon–Fri, 10am–8pm; Sat, 10am–7pm; Sun, 12pm–6pm*

John Lewis

278–306 Oxford Street, W1

(020) 7629 7711

🚇 Bond Street/Oxford Circus

Sensible store, which is 'Never knowingly undersold'. If you need buttons and a bird box under one roof, it's the only place to go.

🕐 *Mon–Wed, 9.30am–7pm; Thu, 9.30am–8pm; Fri–Sat, 9.30am–7pm; Sun, closed*

Liberty

Regent Street, W1

(020) 7734 1234

🚇 Oxford Circus

Liberty opened in 1875, selling ornaments, fabric and objects d'art. It looms over Regent's Street like a giant Liquorice Allsort and is Itchy's fave browse.

🕐 *Mon–Sat, 10am–7pm; Sun, 12pm–6pm*

Marks & Spencer

458 Oxford Street, W1

(020) 7935 7954

🚇 Marble Arch/Bond Street

Tasty food in ritzy plastic containers, ever-improving clothes and more fancy pants than you can shake a stick at.

🕐 *Mon–Fri, 9am–9pm; Sat, 8.30am–7.30pm; Sun, 12pm–6pm*

Selfridges

400 Oxford Street, W1

(0870) 8377377

🚇 Bond Street/Marble Arch

A huge department store with quirky window displays and a full-on fashionista following. Afternoons can soon turn into evenings here.

🕐 *Mon–Fri, 10am–8pm; Sat, 9.30am–8pm; Sun, 12pm–6pm*

UNISEX CLOTHING

All Saints

6 Foubert's Place, W1

(020) 7494 3909

⊖ Oxford Circus

A decent find for men and women who want to look smart yet stylishly dressed down.

Mon–Sat, 10.30am–7pm; Sun, 12pm–6pm

Cyberdog

Unit 145, The Stables Market, Chalk Farm Road, NW1

(020) 7482 2842

⊖ Camden Town/Chalk Farm

If you've ever wanted to see what goes down at your local hardcore fetish club without having actually having to go, drop by here next Saturday afternoon.

Mon–Fri, 11am–6pm; Sat-Sun, 10am–7pm

Dover Street Market

17–18 Dover Street, W1

(020) 7493 4004

⊖ Oxford Circus

This is the coolest market Itchy has ever set foot in. Comme des Garçons have gathered together their favourite designers and stuck a cafe-shaped cherry on top.

Mon–Sat, 11am–6pm

H&M

261–271 Regent Street, W1

(020) 7493 4004

⊖ Oxford Circus

H&M is at its best here in London. The sales are pretty much constant and can get silly. We love that accessories here are cheaper than they are in TopShop

Mon–Sat, 10am–6pm; Sun, 12pm–6pm

TK Maxx

St Johns Road, SW11

(020) 7228 8072

⊖ Clapham Junction (BR)

Massive in the States and getting that way in Britain, this huge discount shop sells designer clothes, shoes and household items at up to 60% off.

Mon–Sat, 10am–6pm; Sun, 12pm–6pm

TopShop/TopMan

214 Oxford Circus, W1

(020) 7636 7700

⊖ Oxford Circus

New to town and need a fresh outfit? Look no further than the shop that is top. Everyone shops here, from plebs to celebs. Don't forget the credit card.

Mon–Sat, 10am–8pm; Sun, 12pm–6pm

Shop

WOMENS' CLOTHING

Agent Provocateur

6 Broadwick Street

(020) 7439 0229

⊖ Oxford Circus/Piccadilly Circus

Saucy underwear that can turn a prim prom queen into Abi Titmuss in seconds.

◉ *Mon–Sat, 11am–7pm*

Urban Outfitters

200–211 Oxford Street

(020)

⊖ Oxford Circus

This hip haven is a shrine to the dedicated follower of fashion. Everything seems to sparkle, so you almost don't resent paying 20 quid for a beaded necklace.

◉ *Mon–Sat, 10am–6pm; Sun, 12pm–6pm*

SHOES

Kurt Geiger

65 South Molton St

(020) 7758 8020

⊖ Bond Street

Alongside its own brand, Kurt Geiger sells a selection of fabulous designer shoes.

◉ *Mon–Sat, 10am–7pm; Sun, 12pm–6pm*

Office

16 Carnaby Street

(020) 7434 2530

⊖ Oxford Circus/Piccadilly Circus

Caters for shoe emergencies and casual browsers with a fine array of boots, shoes and trainers. Here lies everything you need to stay a step ahead of the rest.

◉ *Mon–Sat, 10am–7pm; Sun, 12pm–6pm*

Size

33–34 Carnaby Street

(020) 7287 4016

⊖ Oxford Circus/Piccadilly Circus

If you're into trainers, you'll already know this place. If not, your time will come. Adorning the walls are Polaroid's of customers and every hot trainer going.

◉ *Mon–Sat, 10am–6pm; Sun, 12pm–6pm*

Swear

22 Carnaby Street

(020) 7734 1690

⊖ Oxford Circus/Piccadilly Circus

Rocky, unusual shoes of the type favoured by angst-ridden girl band stars and European exchange students. Will go nicely with your bondage trews.

◉ *Mon–Sat, 11am–7pm; Sun, 2pm–6pm*

SECONDHAND

295

295 Portobello Road, W10

No phone

⊖ Ladbroke Grove/Notting Hill Gate

Classy vintage shop, favoured by the Notting Hill celeb crew. Beat 'em to it..

Ⓦ *Fri–Sat, 8.30am–5pm*

Absolute Vintage

15 Hanbury Street. E1

(020) 7247 3883

⊖ Liverpool Street

There are some clothes to rummage through, but the real draw is the footwear. Colour-coded and reasonably priced, you'll find everything from stilettos to cowboy boots.

Ⓦ *Opening times vary. Call ahead.*

Beyond Retro

110–112 Cheshire Street, E2

(020) 613 3636

⊖ Liverpool Street

In a 5,000-square-foot warehouse just off Brick Lane lies every vintage lover's wet dream (complete with compulsory fusty, damp smell). Rummage-a-go-go.

Ⓦ *Daily, 10am–6pm*

Blackout II

51 Endell Street, WC2

(020) 7240 5006

⊖ Covent Garden

Hip vintage shop in the heart of Covent Garden. Probably better for fancy dress than fashionista finds.

Ⓦ *Mon–Fri, 11am–7pm; Sat, 11.30am–6.30pm; Sun, closed*

Brick Lane shoes

88 Brick Lane, E1

(020) 7247 8571

⊖ Shoreditch/Liverpool Street

At Christmas there was a tree with a hundred vintage shoes in the branches instead of baubles. If that doesn't scream 'cool' then we don't know what does.

Ⓦ *Opening times vary. Call ahead.*

Designer Bargains

29 Kensington Church Street, W8

(020) 7795 6777

⊖ High Street Kensington

This place is like TK Maxx for the rich and famous. You'll still need to take out a second mortgage to buy most things, but hey, it's fashion daahling.

Ⓦ *Mon–Sat, 10am–6pm*

Shop

BOOKS

Blackwell's

100 Charing Cross Road, WC2

(020) 7292 5100

⊖ Tottenham Court Road

Famous book palace. Better suited to those with an academic bent than chick-lit lovers.

🕒 *Mon–Sat, 9.30am–8pm; Sun, 12pm–6pm*

Daunt Books

83 Marylebone High Street, W1

(020) 224 2295

⊖ Bond Street/Baker Street

The ultimate independent bookshop, and one of the most beautiful ones we've ever seen. This place is an Itchy fave for lounging, dreaming and browsing. Aaaaah.

🕒 *Mon–Sat, 9am–7.30pm; Sun, 11am–6pm*

Foyles

119 Charing Cross Road, WC2

(020) 7437 5660

⊖ Tottenham Court Road

A shop with loads of character – the layout is still puzzling (but we're getting better at it by the day). Staff won't look at you funny when you ask if they stock sci-fi porn.

🕒 *Mon–Sat, 9.30am–8pm; Sun, 12pm–6pm*

Oxfam Bookshop

91 Marylebone High Street, W1

(020) 7487 3570

⊖ Bond Street/Baker Street

This shop specializes in books, books and more books. Novels, annuals and vintage magazines from 50p and less draw the punters in their droves.

🕒 *Times vary. Please call ahead.*

Ulysses

40 Museum Street, W1

(020) 7851 2400

⊖ Tottenham Court Road/Holborn

If you get all moist at the prospect of fondling a signed first edition, Ulysses will be a perv's pradise for you. They've got over 20,000 books in stock.

🕒 *Mon–Sat, 10am–6pm*

Waterstones

3–206 Piccadilly, W1

(020) 7851 2400

⊖ Piccadilly Circus

This is also every bookworm's idea of paradise – six floors crammed with classics and all the new releases, plus an art gallery, coffee bar and a gift shop. Joy.

🕒 *Mon–Sat, 10am–6pm; Sun, 12pm–6pm*

MUSIC

Dub Vendor

274 Lavender Hill, SW11

(020) 7223 3757

⊖ Clapham Junction (BR)

Sells reggae and dancehall classics.

🕑 *Mon–Thu, 10am–7pm; Fri, 10am–7.30pm; Sun, 11.30am–5.30pm*

Fopp

1 Earlham Street, W1

(020) 7379 0883

⊖ Leicester Square/Covent Garden

It might be a chain but Fopp's heart is in the right place. An excellent collection of chart and back catalogue records for a tenner, as well as unerringly friendly staff.

🕑 *Mon–Sat, 10am–7pm; Sun, 11am–5pm*

Ray's Jazz at Foyles

113–119 Charing Cross Road, WC2

(020) 7437 5660

⊖ Tottenham Court Road

After years of living in Covent Garden, Ray's Jazz was saved from closure by its move to bookshop Foyles. Which for jazz fans was akin to Jesus meeting that Lazarus bloke.

🕑 *Mon–Sat, 9.30am–7.30pm; Sun, 12pm–6pm*

Rough Trade

16 Neals Yard, WC2

(020) 7240 0105

⊖ Covent Garden

Originally a second-hand shop in Notting Hill, Rough Trade is synonymous with great music. Geoff Travis's record label spawned The Smiths and The Strokes.

🕑 *Mon–Sat, 10am–6pm; Sun, 1pm–5pm,*

Vinyl Junkies

Basement, 9–12 Berwick Streett, W1

(020) 7439 2923

⊖ Oxford Circus

Top destination for DJs and collectors, specialising in cutting-edge house, disco, offbeat, funk, new jazz, abstract, vocals, soul, compilations and rarities.

🕑 *Mon–Sat, 12pm–6pm*

Virgin Megastore

14–19 Oxford Street, W1

(020) 7631 1234

⊖ Tottenham Court Road

You might feel like a corporate whore in the Megastore, but at least you'll find what you're looking for. Unlike Bono.

🕑 *Mon–Sat, 10am–8.30pm; Thu, 10am–9pm; Sun, 12pm–6pm*

Shop

OTHER

Anything Left Handed
57 Brewer Street, W1

(020) 7437 3910

⊖ Piccadilly Circus

Get a corkscrew for your left-handed friend and be the most thoughtful gift-giver ever.

🕲 *Mon–Fri, 10am–6pm; Sat, 10am–5.30pm*

Butler & Wilson
20 South Molton Street, W1

(020) 409 2955

⊖ Bond Street

For the girl who likes all that glitters, Butler & Wilson is like walking through a set of very pearly gates into accessory heaven. Go on, treat yourself nice.

🕲 *Mon–Sat, 10am–6pm; Sun, 12pm–6pm*

G-Room
46 Carnaby Street, W1

(020) 7734 5994

⊖ Oxford Circus/Piccadilly Circus

With its varnished wooden floors and modern art inspired décor, G-Room's flagship store stands proud as a kind of male answer to Urban Outfitters.

🕲 *Mon–Fri, 10am–7pm; Sun, 12pm–6pm*

Play Lounge
19 Beak Street, W1

(020) 7287 7073

⊖ Oxford Circus/Piccadilly Circus

You know those toys that the graphic designers at work always have on their desks? Little manga figurines and 50s robots? This is where they got 'em.

🕲 *Mon–Sat, 10am–6pm*

Tatty Devine
236 Brick Lane, E2

(020) 7434 225

⊖ Shoreditch/Old Street

It's time for Tatty to conquer Soho. This cute boutique is total birthday present heaven. Get yourself a knitted clock bracelet and a natty plectrum necklace.

🕲 *Mon–Sat, 12pm–7pm*

TomTom
42 New Compton Street, WC2

(020) 7240 7909

⊖ Tottenham Court Road

If you dream of decorating your flat in vintage cool, then splash out on one item at TomTom. They specialise in pop art prints and Banksy originals.

🕲 *Times vary. Call ahead.*

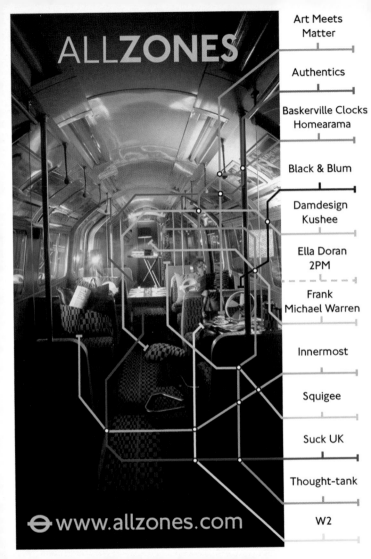

Out & About

STAG&HEN
NIGHTS

BREAK OUT THE L-PLATES AND LOCK UP YOUR DAUGHTERS. HERE'S ITCHY'S GUIDE TO YOUR FINAL NIGHT OF FREEDOM...

Coco De Mer
23 Monmouth Street, WC2
020 7836 8882
⊖ Covent Garden

You're better than that L-plates and knob deely-boppers malarkey. Get yourself some classy clobber at Coco. Anyone for a spanking paddle? Naughty, but nice.

Circus
1 Upper James Street, W1
020 7534 4000
⊖ Piccadilly Circus

A restaurant, smack-bang in the middle of Soho. You can stumble downstairs for a drunken dance-off afterwards.

Alphabet
61–63 Beak Street, W1
020 7439 2190
⊖ Piccadilly Circus

A top-notch cocktail bar for Soho's beautiful people. It's rammed at the weekends, so get yourselves downstairs early for some rampant cocktail action.

Madame Jo-Jo's
8–10 Brewer Street, W1
020 7734 3040
⊖ Piccadilly Circus

Nestled in the seedier part of Soho, this is an open-minded club for discerning funketeers. Dress with taking it all off again in mind and prepare for a night of dancing, posing and flirting - in that order. Watch out for the 'Kitsch Cabaret' nights, which include entry to Sugar Reef as part of the package. The place is usually full to the rafters with an eclectic selection of breakdancers, drag queens and disco dollies – now all you need to do is bring on the dancing girls...

Escapade

150 Camden High Street, NW1
020 7485 7384
⊖ Camden Town

A veritable treasure trove of nonsense. This place is Camden's fancy dress haven, with a joke shop attached to boot. If it's props you're after for the evening, look no further. Whether you need handcuffs, blow-up dolls, rubber boobs, stallion underwear (don't ask), nude playing cards or bondage masks, this is a one-stop-shop for ritual humiliation of any groom-to-be. Before you really go to town, remember, revenge is a dish best served cold...

Mash

19–21 Great Portland Street, W1
0871 332 5892
⊖ Oxford Circus

Book yourselves the green room upstairs and order wood-fired pizzas and specially brewed beer to your hearts' content. You can also order beer taster sticks from the micro-brewery downstairs, which should get the night lubricated nicely. If you get a bit carried away with the prospect of a brewery on site, slide down the bannisters to one of the club nights downstairs. Thanks to a late licence, this place is always heaving with a full-tilt crowd. You wouldn't have it any other way, would you?

Market Place

11 Market Place, W1
020 7079 2020
⊖ Oxford Circus

From the outside, this place looks like a sauna (down, boy). We can assure you it's considerably more fun than being thrashed with twigs by comely Swedish girls in a steamy room... errr... maybe not. Anyway, the beer is cracking and there's a club night downstairs every night of the week. Book yourself one of the alcoves to guarantee a base camp for the evening. Probably best to avoid the Erdinger if you want to stand a fighting chance of getting back up those stairs later.

The Windmill

17-19 Great Windmill Street
020 7439 3558
⊖ Piccadilly Circus

Get down and dirty at one of the capitals oldest strip clubs. Tell the little lady it was like Moulin Rouge.

GIG VENUES

The Forum

9–11 Highgate Road, NW5

0870 534 4444

⊖ Kentish Town

One of London's premier mid-sized venues. Home to all the top touring acts, it always attracts a music-loving crowd. It also hosts all-nighter shindigs for the likes of Mr Scruff and the weekly 'School's Out 4 Ever'. If you're after carnage, you'll be pleased to head that Aussie booze-and-nudity-fest 'The Church' recently moved in.

€ £10–£20

Ronnie Scott's

47 Frith Street, W1

020 7439 0747

⊖ Leicester Square

The most famous jazz club in the country is as electrifying today as it was 50 years ago. Even if you're not a fan of jazzzzz, the intimate, smoky ambience is uniquely seductive. Now home to everyone from Gil Scott Heron to Tom Waits and you can even go salsa dancing upstairs on a Friday. Time to put on that roll neck...

€ £15–£25

Brixton Academy

211 Stockwell Road, SW9

020 7771 3000

⊖ Brixton

The best live venue of its size in London. A former cinema, it attracts the biggest bands, has a fantastic sloping floor so you can see wherever you stand downstairs (as long as the tall bloke with the Afro has gone to the loo), and an atmosphere that could light up most of South London.

€ £15–£25

Shepherd's Bush Empire

Shepherd's Bush Green, W12

0870 771 2000

⊖ Shepherd's Bush

As the venue for Terry Wogan's 1980s TV chat show, the Empire has a special place in Itchy's heart. Since the Old Grey Whistle Test was recorded here, acts from Radiohead to Eminem have filled its opulent rafters and the sound here is rarely bettered – even when you're sitting in the vertigo-inducing balcony.

€ £10–£25

Out & About

CINEMAS

Curzon Soho

93–107 Shaftesbury Avenue, W1
(020) 7439 4805
↔ Leicester Square

Revamped and as luxurious as ever, we love the Curzon Soho. Upstairs there's a great café serving freshly made crêpes smothered in chocolate. Downstairs you'll find a bar where you can sit and talk about the demise of Tom Cruise's career or catch talks and seminars given by directors. They show your more unusual arthouse and European films, have comfy seats and don't let in brats in Kappa tracksuits.

🎬 *Adults, £8.50/£4 (Mon–Thu before 5pm); NUS, £5.50 (Mon–Thu)*

IMAX

1 Charlie Chaplin Walk, SE1
(0870) 787 2525
↔ Waterloo

Take a big game safari or fly to the moon right here in the centre of London, when you take in a movie at the IMAX. The screen's as high as five double decker buses and perhaps because you feel so small, you can't help showing a little bit of childish excitement when you first walk in. It's the largest cinema screen in Britain with a 11,600-watt digital surround-sound system to boot. All of which goes some way to explaining why you'll be so convinced by what you see, you'll be reaching out to touch it, along with everyone else in the audience.

🎬 *Prices vary, but roughly £7*

National Film Theatre

South Bank, SE1
(0871) 223 5655
↔ Waterloo

Although sitting in one of these three screens for a lengthy period of time is akin to taking an uncomfortable plane journey, leg cramps aside, this cinema shows some pretty decent stuff. Specialising in arthouse and repertory work, if you know about film, you'll know of this place's importance soon enough. They also do a nice line in special film seasons and events to keep the buffs happy. Just be sure to walk up and down the aisle every twenty minutes to stave off the deep vein thrombosis.

🎬 *Membership is £15.95 a year, which gets you a pound off every ticket*

Out & About

Prince Charles Cinema

7 Leicester Place, WC2

(020) 7494 3654

⊖ Leicester Square

Famed for its regular Sing-along to the Sound of Music nights, the Charles offers fab membership offers for fans. This is the place to catch the ones you missed a few months, or indeed, a few years ago, plus special screenings of films from around the world. On Feel Good Friday's tickets are just £1 and prices are never more than £4, which laughs in the face of the multiplexes round the corner. They also have some of the comfiest seats in the West End and a screen that's high enough to ensure you can still see when the man with world's biggest head sits down in front of you.

€ £1–£4 (no really)

The Ritzy Cinema

Brixton Oval, SW2

(0870) 755 0062

⊖ Brixton

One of the UK's first purpose built cinemas, the Ritzy is still a contender. Now with free wireless internet in the café downstairs, this is quite the social hang-out in Brixton, dontcha know? Apart from showing films, it's also a jazz club, plus it's comfortable, cosy and welcomes you with a host of snacks and beers. Membership options offer great deals like free screenings, and other stuff includes two Sunday matinees every week, monthly mother and baby screenings (to be avoided) and a Saturday art-fair.

€ £3.50, before 12pm; £7.50, after 5pm; £5, all day Mon

The Screen on Baker Street

96–98 Baker Street, W1

(020) 7935 2772

⊖ Baker Street

With just two screens, going here feels kind of like an old-fashioned trip to the movies, when they dressed up to go and sit in the dark. The largest screen has just 85 seats so you can be forgiven for thinking you've ended up watching a film in someone's living room rather than at a cinema, and you can take a load of yummy stuff in with you, like drinks from their very own bar (in a plastic cup mind). They show a mix of mainstream and less obvious choices, so there's always something you'll want to see.

€ £6 Mon–Fri, before 5.30pm; £8.50 at all other times

Out and about

OUTDOOR SWIMMING

Brockwell Lido

Dulwich Road, SE24

(020) 7274 3088

⊖ Brixton

As an open-air facility involving a large hole full of water in South London, one initially wonders about the cleanliness here. However, snobbery aside, the lido, built in 1937, has become a staple of the community and as well as perfectly hygienic swimming it offers yoga, meditation and other activities in the surrounding buildings. In the summer you'll have to battle the kids for a spot in the sun, but it's a nicely kept little secret amongst the locals.

Mon–Fri, 6.45am–8pm (dependent on weather); Weekends, 12pm–6pm

Hampstead Ponds

Hampstead Heath, NW3

No phone

⊖ Highgate

There has been some debate in recent months over whether to close the ponds to the public, although as it stands you can still swim there, and people do. Every morning. Come rain, snow, fog or shine. Three of them are used for bathing, one's mixed, one for the ladies, and one for the lads. It's almost an alternative social club in the summer. Let's hope they keep it this way, as they have done for hundreds of years. You gotta fight for your right to... errr... swim in murky waters.

£2 per session, £1 for concessions (also subject to protest)

Serpentine

Hyde Park, W2

No phone

⊖ Hyde Park Corner

For more than 100 years, Londoner's have flocked here in the summer months to slurp ice-cream and swim 110 yards of the pool. There's a rumour that there are some oddballs who go for a dip at 9am on Christmas Day, but we don't know anyone prepared to check for us. Open to the sane from June to mid-September and costing £3.50 for adults, it's perfect for an afternoon picnic. Hell, pretend you're in Spain and strip down for the whole day, why not? Gems like this are few and far between in London, so you may as well make the most of it.

Jun–Sep, 10am–6pm

£3.50; Membership, £15 per annum

PARKS

Richmond Park

Bog lodge Yard, TW10

⊖ Richmond

Richmond is a vast expanse of green in one of London's most leafy areas. Popular with cyclists, horse riders and other sporty types. On a wildlife tip, it's also full of deer. Altogether now, 'Doe, a deer...'

Crystal Palace Park

Crystal Palace Road, SE22

⊖ Crystal Palace (BR)

Paxton's hilltop testament to all things Victorian has to be seen. The Palace is long gone but the maze remains along with 33 prehistoric monsters, a concert bowl, a boating lake and a sports arena.

Primrose Hill

Primrose Hill Road, NW3

⊖ Chalk Farm

Panoramic views, the chance to do a bit of celeb-spotting or just somewhere to relax after the jostling of nearby Camden Market; Primrose Hill is close to perfect. Lots of lively pubs and cafes too.

Victoria Park

Approach Road, E2

⊖ Bethnal Green

East London isn't exactly known for its open spaces, but Victoria Park is a green oasis. Large ponds, tea rooms and even a bowling green add to the escapism. Look out for the bendy woman doing her workout.

Out & About

THEATRES

Donmar Warehouse

41 Earlham Street, WC2

(020) 7240 4882

⊖ Covent Garden

Sam Mendes was creative director here for a few years, before American Beauty shot him further to fame, but the Donmar hasn't lost it's reputation for consistently producing high quality, contemporary drama. Most plays have quite short runs so keep checking the website for new arrivals. Last year saw Madonna and Ewan McGregor tread the boards and their knack of pulling big names looks set to continue, so prepare yourself for more stellar turns in 2006.

◉ *Performance times vary*

National Theatre

South Bank, SE1

(020) 7452 3000

⊖ Waterloo

You can't miss the National at night, lighting up the Thames with its dramatic sign. This is London theatre at its best – you know you're experiencing something great even before the curtains go up. There are three theatres in all, running up to seven productions at a time. Book early to get the £10 sponsored tickets. You're pretty much guaranteed a quality performance and on Saturday nights, they open up the riverside terrace for a club night. An added bonus is the fact that the South Bank has become all the more alluring now they've opened more eateries along the river.

◉ *Daily, 9am–11pm*

Regent's Park Open Air Theatre

Inner Circle, Regent's Park, NW1

(08700) 601 811

⊖ Regent's Park

In the summer this place is pure magic. Hosting a variety of plays in the warm months it proves Mother Nature is the perfect backdrop to any production, although it can be funny watching Shakespeare, getting lost in the beauty of olde England and then seeing a plane roar overhead on its way to Heathrow. Don't sit too far back as the sound tends to muffle against any outside noises, and take a cushion as the cheap seats can be uncomfortable after a while. There's a bar, a buffet and you can even bring a picnic. Bliss.

◉ *May–Sep; performance times vary*

COMEDY

Comedy Store

Haymarket House, 1A Oxendon Street, SW1
020 7344 0234
⊖ Piccadilly Circus

Originally located above a strip club in Soho, the Comedy Store has now moved to slightly more reputable surrounds. Boasting the likes of Paul Merton on its line up in the last few weeks, for fans of big name comedy acts, this is the place to go to catch the cream of the British comedy scene at reasonable prices.

Monday Club

Tattershall Castle Street, SW1
0793 2658 895
⊖ Embankment

This little-known gem is one of London's finest comedy nights. Set in the intimate, nigh-on romantic environment of a boat on the Thames, the line-up regularly features some of the best regulars on the London circuit as well as the odd secret show by big name comedians. Shows are fortnightly. Call ahead for the line-up.

Comedy Cafe

66–68 Rivington Street, EC2
020 7739 5706
⊖ Old Street

This big red and yellow building, located in the heart of Shoreditch doesn't just look like Pat Sharpe's Funhouse, but is also one of the few places dishing up humour to the normally oh–so–serious Hoxton residents. Usually consistent in turning out a good line-up, this is rumoured to be the comedians' venue of choice.

Jongleurs

Dingwalls, Camden Lock, NW1
020 7564 2500
⊖ CamdenTown/Chalk Farm

It's the comedy equivalent of Starbucks in terms of the stranglehold that it's acheived on the UK comedy scene, but this doesn't make a night out here any less fun. This particular venue is nicely tucked on the prettier side of Camden Lock, so there's plenty of scope for wayward, late-night rambling afterwards.

Out & About

MUSICALS

Billy Elliot
Victoria Palace Theatre, SW1
(0870) 895 5577
⊖ Victoria

Lavish scenery and moving tunes by Elton, this one's a crowd-pleaser. Try to get last-minute ticket for under £40.

Chicago
Adelphi Theatre, Strand, WC2
(020) 7344 0055
⊖ Charing Cross

With celebs of decreasing levels of fame treading the boards (Darius is in it at the mo) and endless sequins, and high kicks, this still is one of the best shows in town right now.

Jerry Springer, The Opera
Cambridge Theatre, Seven Dials, WC2
(0870) 890 1102
⊖ Covent Garden

Absolutely f**king brilliant, controversial and totally bloody hilarious – just try to spend the time figuring out exactly why thousands of people complained to the BBC when they aired it last year.

Mamma Mia!
Prince Edward, Old Compton Street, W1
(020) 7447 5400
⊖ Leicester Square

Cheese on a stick for *Muriel's Wedding* freaks and Abba fans. This one is packed out with hen nights whooping it up like there's no tomorrow, but we've also heard rumours that Madge has been in recently.

The Producers
Theatre Royal Drury Lane, WC2
(0870) 890 1109
⊖ Covent Garden

If you see one musical this year, make sure it's this one. Mel Brooks' creation and winner of 12 Tony's on its Broadway run. Singalong to *Springtime for Hitler*. Deeply inappropriate, but damn funny.

We Will Rock You
Dominion Theatre, W1
(0870) 534 4444
⊖ Tottenham Court Road

This show gets constant standing ovations and is always packed out, so get yourself a ticket and join the party. Including 24 of Queen's greatest hits, they bring house down, night after night.

FESTIVALS

London Film Festival

It may not have the glitz of Cannes, but the London Film Festival is still one of the world's best, showcasing the wide range of World Cinema Sure, the big Hollywood movies turn up with their inevitable stars and entourages, but the real fun lies in discovering the hidden gems.

Meltdown

For one month each summer, a celeb curator schedules a series of shows at the Royal Festival Hall. Previous hosts, such as Morrissey and Nick Cave, have created an event where legends' imaginations run riot in an eclectic mix of music and performance.

Notting Hill Carnival

Still one of the biggest draws of the year in the capital, despite the crowds being packed in like sardines. Caribbean colour, goat curry and sound systems audible in Hackney are the order of the day in Europe's largest celebration of Afro-Caribbean culture.

Pride in the Park

The UK's largest gay festival has become a major tourist draw. The colourful parade leads into one of the capital's largest summer parties, with themed bars and a live entertainment stage hosting the latest pop muppets to top the charts... and probably Erasure.

Out & About

GALLERIES

Frith Street Gallery

59–60 Frith Street, W1

(020) 7494 1550

⊖ Tottenham Court Road

This relatively small gallery takes part in art fairs all over the world but occupies a 166-square-metre space over two buildings on Frith Street. They have several showcase rooms of 17th and 19th-century design, as well as a number of exhibitions of painting, sculpture, photography, film and even video. They also represent 21 up-and-coming artists, so you might be able to spot a future star. A great idle half-hour, if you're passing.

☻ *Tue–Fri, 10am–6pm; Sat, 11am–4pm*

ICA

The Mall, SW1

(020) 7930 3647

⊖ Charing Cross

The Institute of Contemporary Arts has made its name amongst the art crowd as one of the most exciting places to gather. The pumping bar area offers great food and usually teems with arty youths all mingling over beers and discussing what films and exhibitions, from the weird to the wonderful, they've just been to see. You can feel the buzz outside on the Mall when something good is happening inside. Make a day and a night of it.

☻ *Mon, 12pm–10.30pm; Tue–Sat, 12pm–1am; Sun, 12pm–11pm*

🆔 *Day membership, £1.50–2.50*

National Portrait Gallery

St Martin's Place. WC2

(020) 7312 2463

⊖ Leicester Square/Charing Cross

You'll feel a childish need to slide down the massive, two-storey escalator in here. It's just humongous, but try to restrain yourself. Instead, go right to the top and check out the Tudor portraits – the only thing older is your gran. Since 1856 the NPG has been home to the portraits of all manner of historical British figures. Charlotte Bronte's even in here, painted by her brother. It'll take you a while to see it all, but it's definitely worth it so save it as a weekend winter warming option and indulge the art-lover in you.

☻ *Daily, 10am–6pm*

Photographer's Gallery

5 & 8 Great Newport Street, WC2

(020) 7831 1772

⊖ Covent Garden

Get some tips from the pro's on how to use that new digital camera when you visit the UK's first independent photographic gallery. Being free to get in makes it a perfect rainy day escape if you're at a loss for something to do in central London. Split over two sites, one hosts exhibitions and a huge, fabulously stocked book shop, and the other hosts the gallery and a café. Exhibitions change frequently so always worth a stop-in if you're passing. They also sell prints upstairs, if you need to get a birthday present.

Mon–Sat, 11am–6pm; Sun, 12pm–6pm

RIBA & café

66 Portland Place, W1

(020) 7580 5533

⊖ Great Portland Street

That's the Royal Institute of British Architects, for those of you not in the know. And not just a wall to wall display of boring buildings either – far from it. This is a fascinating insight to the world of architecture and the café on the first floor (city secret; light, airy and decent value for the cracking food on offer), attracts architects and visitors from near and far. Planning a renovation or a personal 'Changing Rooms' Gothic-cum-rococo interior attempt? Probably best to flick through some of the books on sale in the shop.

Mon–Fri, 8am–6pm; Sat, 9am–5pm

Tate Britain

Millbank, SW1

(020) 7887 8000

⊖ Pimlico

When it first opened its doors in 1897, the art in the Tate was by no means modern. Well, you know what we mean. Now it's got over 65,000 works of art, from photography to installations, and attracts thousands of visitors every week. It hosts the world's biggest collection of work by JMW Turner, British works from 1500 to the present day and 20th-century works by both British and international artists. Culture vultures will have a field day, and if you haven't had enough, they can hop on a Damien Hirst boat down the Thames to Tate Modern.

Sun–Thu, 10am–6pm; Fri–Sat, 10am–10pm

Out & About

MUSEUMS

British Museum
Great Russell Street, WC1
(020) 7636 1555
⊖ Tottenham Court Road/Holborn

The world under one roof and the greatest museum on the planet. Check out the controversial Elgin Marbles while they're still there (be prepared – they're not actual marbles, but impressive slabs of marble art) as well as countless other priceless artefacts. When you get bored of the past, take refuge in the amazing Great Court or soak up the hush of the beautiful Reading Room.

Ο Galleries, Sat–Wed, 10am–5.30pm; Thu–Fri, 10am–8.30pm; Great Court, Sun–Wed 9am–6pm; Thu–Sat, 9am–11pm

V&A
Cromwell Road, SW7
(020) 7938 8500
⊖ South Kensington

This is the connoisseurs design collection. It's firmly on the hip list, with exhibitions from the likes of Vivienne Westwood and bizarre soundscape installations in collaboration with Bjork. Itchy has had the right royal pleasure of rocking out in the courtyard at the summer garden parties (and leaping about in the fountain to live bands too), so keep an eye out on the website for future events. They're usually sponsored by some kind of booze-meister too. Huzzah! We heart galleries that like to blow the cobwebs off now and again.

Ο Mon–Sat, 10am–5.30pm; Sun, 11am–5.50pm

Wallace Collection
Hertford House, Manchester Square, W1
(020) 7563 9500
⊖ Bond Street

If you need to impress someone or just want to rest your weary pins after a shopping marathon in Selfridges, duck onto Manchester Square and check out one of the world's finest privately owned collections of fine art. Paintings, furniture, porcelain and bloody great suits of armour are all to be found here, and of course, they've got a courtyard cafe out back. The coffee isn't exactly cheap, but there's no entry fee to the collection, so get yourself a slab of cake and make like Marie Antoinette.

Ο Daily, 10am–5pm

PUB QUIZZES

QUESTION NUMBER ONE: WHERE CAN I FIND A TAXING PUB QUIZ IN THE MIDST OF THE HEAVING METROPOLIS? (BONUS POINTS WILL BE AWARDED FOR BAR-RELATED PRIZES.)

The Pineapple

51 Leverton Street, NW5

⊖ Kentish Town

Mondays 8.30pm, £1 per head

A quiet Kentish Town local, combining cosy charm with a swanky restaurant and a surprisingly tough pub quiz every Monday night. With 40 general knowledge questions and an obligatory picture round, you'll soon be bitching about the team next to you (particularly as the place is so small they'll have nicked half your answers).

Latchmere

503 Battersea Park Road, SW11

⊖ Clapham Junction (BR)

Thursdays 9pm, £1 per person

Now, this pub quiz has form. Voted Best Pub Quiz in London by the Evening Standard a couple of years ago, the beer round (which offers you the opportunity to win up to four free drinks) never fails to grab our attention. With sweets for last place and no intermediate prizes, this is one quiz with a serious sense of humour.

Frog and Forget-Me-Not

Clapham Common, SW4

⊖ Clapham Common

Tuesdays 8.30pm, Free entry

Every Tuesday, this Clapham Common haunt plays host to a cracking quiz with no limit on team size, which is handy for those latecomers. Get there no later than 7.30pm, as the place soon gets packed out. And while you wait to pick up your prize money you can indulge in the excellent green Thai curry. Might even make you a hot favourite. Boom-boom.

Bushranger

Goldhawk Road, W12

⊖ Shepherd's Bush

Wednesdays 8.30pm, £1.50 per person

A friendly, cosmopolitan crowd makes new faces very welcome at this all singing, all-dancing quiz. Take in music rounds, an 'against the clock' bonus round and an accumulator cash question, where you can win a pot of beer tokens. With prizes ranging from alcohol to local football tickets (QPR sadly), it's worth a trip to the wild west.

A SPORTING CHANCE

Ice skating at Somerset House

London's original and most beautiful ice rink is now an almost iconic part of winter, running from the end of November to the end of January. Indeed if you don't go you'll start to feel like a social pariah. You can't get a more spectacular setting for falling on your ass and night time sees flaming torches and a flood-lit building. Beware: your ankles will be screaming the next day.

The dogs at Walthamstow & Wimbledon

Nothing gets the heart racing like a daft gamble. A night at the dogs is a London must, with both tracks packed with sheepskin-clad characters chattering about form and which greyhound they're thinking of buying. To us, of course, it's just a bit of fun with your mates. Unless you've just stuck your wages on a blind dog with three legs. In which case, your heart'll really be racing.

Lord's and The Oval

Since England finally won the Ashes at The Oval last summer, cricket is the new rock'n'roll, so what better way of spending a summer day, than at the home of cricket or its more rowdy South London counterpart? Also the home grounds of Middlesex and Surrey respectively, your day out could well focus on attempting to explain a googly at the many bars and taverns nearby. That's if you're lucky enough to get a ticket.

The London Marathon

The masochistic among you will need to apply months in advance to even stand a chance of making it onto the list of people allowed to take part. But those of you who prefer to take a more leisurely approach to sport can still take the opportunity to join the crowds of Londoners who assemble to watch the collection of costumed chancers and professional athletes with something to prove. Poor sods. Fancy another pint?

FOOTBALL

WITH SOME OF THE FIERCEST LOCAL RIVALRIES IN THE COUNTRY, LONDON'S DEFINITELY THE PLACE TO WATCH THE BEAUTIFUL GAME.

Chelsea

Stamford Bridge, Fulham Road, SW6
020 7386 7799
⊖ Fulham Broadway

50 years after they last won the championship, Mourinho's boys romped to last year's Premiership title and look to be doing the same this year. Almost as renowned for their charismatic manager as they are for their superstars, they at least still have an English core team.

POST-MATCH PINT: Nearby pubs are very much home fans only.

Arsenal

Highbury Stadium, Avenell Road, N5
020 7704 4040
⊖ Arsenal

As we go to print, the Gunners are currently having a rocky final season at their historic Highbury stadium. The move to a new stadium at Ashburton Grove has led to stretched finances and a weakened squad. At least Henry's still around to supply the flair.

POST-MATCH PINT: The Marquess Tavern on Canonbury Road.

Tottenham Hotspur

White Hart Lane, High Road, N17
020 8365 5050
⊖ Seven Sisters

Since the Double of 1961, Tottenham have had scant success other than in the cup. Thankfully for Spurs fans, current manager Martin Jol is creating a team of young English talent that may even bring them Champions League football. Just don't mention Christian Gross.

POST-MATCH PINT: The Park, ten minutes walk from the stadium.

West Ham United

Upton Park, Green Street, E13
020 8548 2700
⊖ Upton Park (BR)

Despite a famously passionate support behind them, the Hammers have yo-yoed between the top two divisions for years. Now back in the Premiership, the current team has a pleasing blend of quality veterans and exciting young talent.

POST-MATCH PINT: Stadium beer. Local pubs are for home fans only.

TOURS

COME WITH ITCHY ON A GUIDED TOUR OF THE BIG SMOKE. COR BLIMEY COBBLERS, WE'LL HAVE YOU DOING THE LAMBETH WALK IN NO TIME.

London Walks

The best way to take in the capital's colourful history is to hit the streets. For the best guided walks around London, check out the aptly-titled London.walks.com, a mish–mash of historical strolls including 'Shakespeare's London', the illicit-sounding 'Legal and Illegal London' not to mention the infamous 'Jack The Ripper' tour, which is genuinely chilling. History, naughtiness and foul play. Sounds like a normal night out to us.

The Duck Tour

It sounds quite bizarre, and that's because it is. You take a normal bus tour past some of London's historic sites – the London Eye, Westminster etc – before the amphibious vehicle you're in suddenly launches itself into the Thames for a 70-minute trip down the river, which remains the greatest way to see the city. You might think it all sounds very James Bond, but this yellow tank is simply surreal. Big night out beforehand and you'll think you're tripping.

The London Eye

The one decent thing to come out of London's sparkling millennium celebrations, (we won't mention that carcass in Greenwich), the Eye has rapidly become our number one tourist attraction. And it's certainly an amazing feat of engineering. Well worth doing once to say you've been; make sure you go at dusk to get the best view (just as London starts to light up). Itchy wanted it to go a bit faster, like a real Ferris wheel.

Silver Sturgeon Boat Parties

Booze-fuelled parties on boats? Obviously a great idea, particularly when they're full of trendy Hoxtonites vomiting over their new vintage trainers. It's all fun and games on the Silver Sturgeon, which hosts shindigs of all sorts. You can hire the 61-metre river cruiser for whatever type of event you so desire, allowing you and your friends to get tanked up in the faux art-deco interior. All aboard...

Itchy

CALLING ALL ASPIRING JOURNALISTS...

We need daring writers to contribute their sparkling talents to the next issue of Itchy magazine.

We want the inside track on the bars, pubs, clubs and restaurants in your city, as well as longer features and dynamic pictures to represent the comedy, art, music, theatre, cinema and sport scenes in your city.

If you're interested in getting involved, please send examples of your writing to: editor@itchymedia. co.uk, clearly stating which city you can work in. All work will be fully credited.

Bath/Birmingham/Brighton/Bristol/Cardiff/Edinburgh/Glasgow/ Leeds/Liverpool/London/Manchester/Nottingham/ Oxford/Sheffield/York

Laters

Laters

LATE-NIGHT VENUES

101

101 New Oxford Street, WC1

(020) 7379 3112

⊖ Tottenham Court Road

Rarely have we witnessed an establishment so hateful or horrible. Not only is it stuck under the malevolent hulk of concrete that is the Centre Point, it also has surly staff, a hideous décor and a crowd that wouldn't know subtlety if it hit them in the face with a crowbar. And the fact that most of them are tourists is no excuse for such inhumanity. Do what we did and use it purely to urinate in before you get the night bus. It deserves no more.

ⓦ *Mon–Sat, 10am–2.30am*

Balans

60 Old Compton Street, W1

(020) 7439 2183

⊖ Leicester Square

Not surprisingly for a bar on Old Compton Street, Balans has a largely gay crowd, but everyone is welcome to stay here until the early hours. And that means early: normal kicking out time is around 5am. With tables crammed in tightly, the atmosphere is always fairly lively. They do some excellent Mexican food and sticky desserts, and frankly, anywhere that does a cocktail called 'Weeping Jesus' deserves a mention.

ⓦ *Mon–Thu, 8am–5am; Fri–Sat, 8am–6am; Sun, 8am–2am*

ⓦ *Quesadilla, £6.75*

ⓦ *£10.95*

Bar Italia

22 Frith Street, W1

(020) 7437 4520

⊖ Leicester Square

Dragging yourself and your good-for-nothing mates from the night's last drinking den, the hunger has hit home and things ain't looking pretty. The impulse for kebab might be strong but this is a much more civilised way of ending an uncivilised evening. On Saturday nights, the sports screen turns into a karaoke guide, with the whole place singing at full tilt. Grab a stool and a coffee, and watch Soho's prettiest boys and girls to your heart's content until the sun comes up. Bar Italia, we love you and we want to have your babies.

ⓦ *Daily, 24 hours*

Costa Dorado

47–55 Hanway Street, W1

(020) 7636 7139

⊖ Tottenham Court Road

Late night Spanish bar on the legendary Hanway Street and home to countless scenes of devastation on a scale that's almost unimaginable. This neat little restaurant (check out the excellent paella) turns into a cacophony of shrieking girls and boys after hours, with live guitars and flamenco floor shows involving men called Miguel until about three in the morning. It might sound like an absolute nightmare, but believe us, it's fun and always a damn funny one to figure out the next morning.

◉ *Mon–Sat, 6pm–3am*

Elbow Rooms

89–91 Chapel Market, N1

(020) 7278 3244

⊖ Angel

The potential for inebriation – and ensuing misdemeanours – offered by the Elbow Rooms is so vast, that Itchy was once escorted from the premises and asked not to come back, at least for the rest of that night. But they only have themselves to blame really. Tucked away on Chapel Market, the home of such iniquity might seem a little too clinically decorated for sensitive souls and yet the late night boozing, pool and quality music choices almost make up for its soulless interior.

◉ *Mon, 6pm–2am; Tue–Thu, 12pm–2am; Fri–Sat, 12pm–3am; Sun, 12pm–10.30pm*

GE Club

Great Eastern Hotel, 40 Liverpool Street, EC2

(020) 7618 5000

⊖ Liverpool Street

As host to the 'Return To New York' club night, Terence Conran's bar at the Great Eastern Hotel became synonymous with uber-cool music, Kate Moss and the general glitterati. A lot calmer then you'd think it might be, it's a great place to have a quiet late-night booze in classy surroundings. Mind you, when this lot decide to throw a party, this place really rocks. The DJs are usually of the Soulwax persuasion, so expect Dolly P vs 50 Cent. Your only problem might be persuading the bouncers to let you in. Best scrub up fancy first.

◉ *Varies according to club nights*

Harlem

78 Westbourne Grove, W2

(020) 7985 0900

Bayswater/Notting Hill Gate/Royal Oak

All the way from New York, courtesy of the legendary Arthur Baker, comes Harlem: one of those places that likes to be everything to everyone. 'Oooo, tonight Matthew, I'm going to be a bar. No, a restaurant. No, a diner! No, a club. No ...' You get the picture. Whatever this place decides to be, it's a cracker. Wicked soul food (fried chicken that doesn't come in a bucket), funky choons and it's open 'til two ay em. High five, brother.

Mon–Sat, 10.30am–2am;

Sun, 10.30am–12am

Eggs benedict, £7.50

£15

The Pit at The Old Vic

The Cut

(020) 7928 2975

Waterloo

The restaurant and bar at the Old Vic theatre is fast becoming a late-night haunt for avid theatre-goers and local foodies alike. While the restaurant is open until 9pm, the bar kicks on until 2am, Thursday to Saturday. It's something of a well-kept secret at the mo, but more and more people are getting wind. Itchy should warn you that starting up a singsong on the grand piano is probably ill-advised. Other than that, it's the perfect place for an after-hours glass of red in civilised surroundings.

Mon–Wed, 12pm–12am;

Tue–Sat, 12pm–2am

The Hope

94 Cowcross Street, EC1

(020) 7253 8525

Farringdon

A traditional Smithfield's pub which still has close links to the meat market (but not in the same way as Infernos in Clapham), hence its 6am opening time. However, you should probably beware of the fact that they won't serve you if you're already half-cut. Along with the range of pleasingly big, meaty sandwiches, the Sirloin Restaurant is upstairs for a hefty meal. The interior is ultra-cosy, so it's perfect for those winter mornings, trying to make your way back from Fabric. Get yourself a sheepskin coat and practice your market banter.

Mon–Sat, 6am–8.30pm

Soho Arts Club

50 Frith Street, W1

(020) 7287 9236

Leicester Square

Broken glass and flailing limbs are the constants in this most shambolic of London nightclubs, tucked away off a dark Soho street. Seasoned Arts Club regulars will take up residence on the seats available, while the rest of the scrum get busy on the dancefloor. The DJ looks like he used to be in Def Leppard and before you know it, you'll be waving your hands in the air to *Living on a Prayer,* along with the rest of the drunken loons. Keep an eye out for the man who looks like he has rickets and 'The Professor' – a ridiculously overqualified mini cab driver.

Check for specific club night details

THE MORNING AFTER
THE NIGHT BEFORE

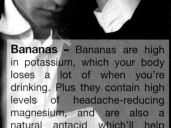

LATE NIGHT DRINKING'S ALL WELL AND GOOD, BUT WAKING UP THE MORNING AFTER RARELY IS. WITH A BIT OF FORETHOUGHT YOU CAN AVOID A LOT OF PAIN. SO, AS YOU'RE STAGGERING HOME AND THE LIGHT OF THAT LATE-NIGHT SHOP SWIMS INTO FOCUS, GET IN THERE AND GRAB SOME OF THE FOLLOWING ITEMS TO MAKE YOURSELF FEEL BETTER:

Fruit juice – Fruit juice contains a good measure of fructose which, helps to burn up alcohol. And it counts as a portion of fruit and veg, so you can repair some of the previous night's damage. Less healthily, you could also pick up one of any number of sugary treats such as Mars bars or sweets. The sugar in them should have the same effect.

Beans – Beans, along with rice, grains, cereals, peas & nuts have high levels of Vitamin B1, or Thiamine, which helps you metabolise booze. It also stabilises the nervous system, as it's a lack of B1, which often causes the shakes.

Bananas – Bananas are high in potassium, which your body loses a lot of when you're drinking. Plus they contain high levels of headache-reducing magnesium, and are also a natural antacid which'll help with the nausea.

Sports cordial – All the toilet trips you'll have made while drunk will have robbed your body of all its salts, so you'll need the salts contained in sports drinks to redress the balance.

Eggs – Eggs contain cysteine, which is used by the body to mop up chemicals called free radicals Sounds a bit scientific, but it'll sort you out right proper.

Tomatoes – Full of antioxidants and vitamins, you should feel better about 15 minutes after eating them. Tomato juice works just as well. Alternatively, add vodka for a 'hair of the dog' style Bloody Mary.

Body

TURKISH BATHS

Ironmonger Row Baths

Ironmonger Row, EC1

⊖ Old Street

020 7253 4011

One of the capital's oldest surviving Victorian turkish baths, the Ironmonger Row baths come complete steam room, hot rooms, icy plunge pool and marble slabs for massages. They also have a relaxation area, featuring beds for you to lie down on and have a snooze after the stress of lounging around in a spaaaaah.

York Hall

Old Ford Road, E2

⊖ Bethnal Green

0208 980 2243

York Hall features one of Europe's largest surviving Victorian baths, and following a vigorous local campaign to save the baths from closure, they're now open for the foreseeable future. Head on down and take advantage of the hot rooms, while reflecting on the antics that the Krays must have got up to in here. Ooo-errr.

The Porchester Centre

Queensway, W2

⊖ Bayswater

020 7792 2919

Despite the history surrounding this place, the interior of this place has been brought well and truly into the 21st century. The sandy-coloured walls, archways and statuettes provide a relaxing ambience for the men's, womens and mixed couples sessions that are run here. It's also the site of some epic parties, so keep 'em peeled for late night action.

The Sanctuary

12 Floral Street, WC2

⊖ Covent Garden

0870 770 3350

For those of you who are bothered about how modern their relaxation techniques are, the Sanctuary is the place to head to. There's a steam room, sauna, sanarium as well as an atrium pool featuring the kind of swing that Pamela Anderson and Tommy Lee famously used for their own kind of 'pampering'. (Down, boy.)

Body

HAIRDRESSERS

Aveda

174 High Holborn, WC1

(020) 7759 7355

⊖ Holborn

It's not who you know, it's who does your hair. Will leave your whole head smiling.

◉ *Mon–Fri, 9.30am–7pm; Sat, 9am–6.30pm*

Fish

30 D'arblay Street, W1

(020) 7494 2398

⊖ Leicester Square

Zoe Ball, Paul Weller and Johnny Vaughan all vouch for the fact that the Fish hair-cutting experience is well above average. Try the fish-finger styling product.

◉ *Mon–Fri, 10am–7pm; Sat, 10am–6.30pm*

Hair by Fairy

8–10 Neal's Yard, WC2

(020) 7497 0776

⊖ Covent Garden

A young and creative team of hair stylists. The salon is unisex and you don't need to make an appointment.

◉ *Mon–Wed & Sat, 10am–6pm; Thu–Fri, 10am–7pm; Sun, 12pm–5pm*

Tommy Guns

65 Beak Street, W1

(020) 7439 0777

⊖ Leicester Square

Don't take them up on too many beers and cocktails when you rest your bum in the barber's chair – or before you know it you'll be agreeing to purple highlights.

◉ *Mon–Fri, 10am–7pm; Sat, 10am–6pm*

SPA

DON'T SAY WE DON'T TREAT YOU RIGHT...

Mandarin Oriental

66 Knightsbridge, SW1

020 7235 2000

⊖ Knightsbridge

Inspired by ancient cultures and their attempt to live in balance with the rhythms of nature, Mandarin Oriental is the place for anyone with a dodgy hippy past. Or a trust fund.

Elemis Day Spa

2–3 Lancashire Court, W1

0870 410 4220

⊖ Bond Street

If you're after a bit of pampering, why not head to Europe's leading day spa? If it's good enough for Gwyneth Paltrow and Sophie Dahl, it's good enough for you.

The Refinery

60 Brook Street, W1

020 7409 2001

⊖ Bond Street

The refinery is one of the capital's few male-only Spas, so now metrosexuals can indulge themself in a little pampering too. And no, we won't cast aspersions on your sexuality...

Agua at the Sanderson

50 Berners Street, W1

020 7300 1400

⊖ Oxford Circus

Milk, honey and sesame oil: no, not a bedtime drink, but the signature massage oils here. Sounds nice, but at £73 for 55 minutes, prepare to shell out for the pleasure.

Body

GYMS

Fitness First
Various locations
(0870) 898 80 80
You can't go far in London without spotting one of these, beckoning you and your bulges inside. State-of-the-art equipment makes exercise bearable.

Third Space
13 Sherwood Street, W1
(020) 7439 7333
⊖ Piccadilly Circus
Truly swank city, this is the Brad and Angelina of the gym world. Offering over 30 classes, a swimming pool, wi-fi membership, dry-cleaning, a live DJ, personal training and much more.

Triyoga
6 Erskine Road, NW3
(020) 7483 3344
⊖ Chalk Farm
If you're really serious about bending and stretching your way to a better 'you', ask any one of Primrose Hill's enthusiasts to convince you that yoga is not just for ultra-supple celebrities.

OTHER

The Floatworks
1 Thrale Street, SE1
(020) 7357 011
⊖ London Bridge
What do you get when you cross 700lbs of Epsom salts with 170 gallons of water? Total bliss, that's what.

Walk-in Backrub
14 Neal's Yard, WC2
(020) 7836 9111
⊖ Covent Garden
There are five of these in London but the original sits tucked away in Neal's Yard. With a ten-minute back rub at under a tenner, it's a treat if your shopping bags have done your back in.

Zulu Tattoos & Metalmorphoses
In Selfridges, 400 Oxford Street, W1
(020) 7318 3801
⊖ Bond Street
This will probably be the most expensive tattoo you're ever likely to get, but after truly professional treatment, it'll be a multi-coloured result to treasure.

Sleep

Sleep

EXPENSIVE ACCOMMODATION

Hazlitt's
6 Frith Street, W1
(020) 7434 1771
⊖ Tottenham Court Road
A laid-back literary haunt.
❂ *Doubles from £175 per night*

Malmaison Hotel
Charterhouse Square, EC1
(020) 7012 3700
⊖ Farringdon
There are several of these around London. This one is a converted nursing home with 97 rooms – perfect for the an after party for Shoreditch players.
❂ *Doubles from £68 per person*

The Rookery
Cowcross Street, EC1
(020) 7336 0931
⊖ Farringdon
Check into the past here and discover London's best-kept secret in the hotel world. The atmosphere is that of the luxury home you never had. Sublime.
❂ *Doubles from £175 per night*

Sanderson
50 Berners Street, W1
(020) 7300 1400
⊖ Tottenham Court Road
An urban retreat, you'll need a second mortgage just to stay here. Step inside the purple bar where the celeb's sip vodka and discuss their Prada purchases.
❂ *Doubles from £215 per night*

Savoy
The Strand, WC2
(020) 7836 4343
⊖ Charing Cross
Old-school glamour, with a bar, a restaurant, a roof-top swimming pool, full-service spa, piano-accompanied afternoon tea and evening cocktails.
❂ *Doubles from £230; breakfast not included*

The Zetter
86–88 Clerkenwell Road, EC1
(020) 7324 4444
⊖ Farringdon
Cute floral-pattered furniture and comfy, fluffy rugs make the rooms irresistible, while the trendy, red, spiral staircase is just begging you to slide down it.
❂ *Doubles from £119*

MID-RANGE ACCOMMODATION

Columbia Hotel

95–99 Lancaster Gate, W2

(020) 7402 0021

⊖ Lancaster Gate

Rock'n'roll hotel. Vodka-on-your-cornflakes.

✪ *Doubles from £86 per night*

Days Inn Westminster

82–86 Belgrave Road, SW1

(020) 7828 8661

⊖ Victoria

With 82 simply furnished rooms, it's hardly the height of luxury here, but with 24-hour reception cover and internet access, it's a great choice for the location alone.

✪ *Doubles from £38 per night*

Mad Hatter Hotel

3–7 Stamford Street, SE1

(020) 7401 9222

⊖ Waterloo

Cute and brimming with history, this small hotel is the perfect place to dump the relatives. It's a quick walk away from the Tate and the National Theatre.

✪ *Doubles from £86 per night*

The Montague

15 Montague Street, WC1

(020) 7637 1001

⊖ Tottenham Court Road

This hotel is nine Georgian town houses joined together. It's the perfect retreat for your mum when she comes to stay, with the British Museum around the corner.

✪ *Doubles from £180 per night*

Ramada Jarvis Hyde Park

150 Bayswater Road, W2

(08457) 303 040

⊖ Queensway

This is a strange and quirky hotel. (That's another way of saying the décor is naff.) But still, for the location (overlooking Hyde Park) you really have to check it out.

✪ *Doubles from £59 per person*

St Giles Hotel

Bedford Avenue, WC1

(020) 7300 3000

⊖ Tottenham Court Road

Right in the heart of the West End, this is the place to go to if your drunken friend suggests getting a room instead of a cab ride back home.

✪ *Doubles from £79 per night*

CHEAP ACCOMMODATION

Ashlee House

261–265 Grays Inn Road, WC1

(020) 7833 9400

⊖ King's Cross

Only a two-minute walk from Kings Cross, backpackers head here in their droves.

☉ *Dorm bed from £14 per night*

Barry House Hotel

12 Sussex Place, Hyde Park, W2

(020) 7723 7340

⊖ Bond Street

This family-run hotel near Marble Arch offers incredibly warm hospitality and a cosy stay in an historic setting. A great location for summer strolling.

☉ *Double room from £65 per night*

easyHotel

14 Lexham Gardens, Kensington. W8

Phone booking not available

⊖ Gloucester Road

There's nothing luxurious about this hotel except, perhaps the location. Bring your sunglasses. Your room is going to be orange. You gets what you pays for...

☉ *Double room from £25 per night*

Gower House Hotel

57 Gower Street, WC1

(020) 7636 4685

⊖ Goodge Street

In a terrace of Georgian town houses in Bloomsbury, this listed building is comfortably furnished. It's also a darn good location for shopping sprees.

☉ *Double room from £50 per night*

Ibis

47 Lillie Road, Earl's Court, SW6

(020) 7610 0880

⊖ Earl's Court

With almost 500 rooms, this is pretty standard budget stuff. They've got live music every night, although we can't vouch for its quality. Cheap'n'cheerful.

☉ *Double room from £59 per night*

St Christopher's Inns hostel

48–50 Camden High Street, NW1

(020) 7407 1856

⊖ Camden Town

If you're in London for some fun, you won't want to miss a night in Camden. Breakfast is included, so your hangover will thank you as well as your wallet.

☉ *Dorm bed from £9.50 per night*

St Pancras/Holland Park YHA

78–81 Euston Road, NW1/Holland Park, W8

(020) 7388 9998 (St Pancras)

(020) 7937 0748 (Holland Park)

⊖ King's Cross/Holland Park

Several locations. Itchy wants to live in the hostel in the middle of Holland Park

☉ *Dorm bed from £24 per night*

University of London Halls

Various locations around the centre of London

(020) 7862 8880

A lot of universities offer their halls of residence to people other than students out of term time. Snuggle down and regress to that special moment when you tried to fit two people in the narrow bed.

☉ *Room between £20–30 per night*

Itchy

WHERE CAN YOU BUY YOUR GLASS SLIPPERS, AND AVOID TURNING INTO A PUMPKIN?

MAKE EVERY NIGHT A FAIRY TALE. THE ITCHY GUIDE IS THE INSIDERS' GUIDE, TELLING YOU WHERE TO GO TO MEET PRINCE CHARMING AND HOW TO AVOID THE UGLY SISTERS IN 16 UK CITIES.

Bath, Birmingham, Brighton, Bristol, Cambridge, Cardiff, Edinburgh, Glasgow, Leeds, Liverpool, London, Manchester, Nottingham, Oxford, Sheffield, York.

Useful info

Useful info

TAXIS

Addison Lee
(020) 7387 8888

Freedom Cabs
(020) 7734 1313

Lady Cabs
(020) 7272 3300

Radio Cabs
(020) 7272 0272

CAR HIRE

Budget
(0800) 181181

TRAINS

Connex South Central
(08706) 030405

Eurostar
(0870) 518 6186

First Great Western
(08457) 000125

GNER
(08457) 225 225

National Rail Enquiries
(08457) 484 950

Virgin Trains
(08457) 222 333

TRAVEL

Catamaran Cruises
(020) 7987 1185

London Transport Info Line
(020) 7222 1234

London Transport Lost Property Office
200 Baker Street, NW1
(0845) 330 9882
⊖ Baker Street
◉ Mon–Fri 8.30am–4pm

Victoria Coach Station
164 Buckingham Palace Road, SW1
(020) 7730 3466
⊖ Victoria

PLANES

Gatwick
(0870) 000 2468
⊖ Victoria (Gatwick Express)

Heathrow
(0870) 000 0123
⊖ Heathrow Terminals 1,2, 3/Heathrow Terminal 4/
Paddington (Heathrow Express)

London City
(020) 7646 0088
⊖ London City Airport (DLR)

Stansted
(0870) 000 0303
⊖ Liverpool Street/Tottenham Hale BR
(Stansted Express)

Useful info

FOOD DELIVERY

Deliverance
(0800) 019 1111
Freshly cooked delivery service.

Leaping Salmon
(0870) 701 9100
DIY food kits for lazy chefs.

ORIENTAL DELIVERY

Feng Sushi – branches
Fulham Road, SW6
(020) 7795 1900

London Bridge, SE1
(020) 7407 8744

PIZZA DELIVERY

Basilico – branches
175 Lavender Hill, SW15
(0800) 389 9770
Wood-fired pizzas with fresh toppings,
made in minutes for your salivating chops.

690 Fulham Road, SW6
(0800) 028 3531

515 Finchley Road, NW3
(0800) 316 2656

178 Upper Richmond Road West, SW14
(0800) 096 8202

26 Penton Street, N1
(0800) 093 4224

Domino's Pizza – branches
89 Charlwood Street, SW1
(020) 7834 2211
Might be a chain, but they come up trumps.

11a Islington High Street, N1
(020) 7713 0707

157 Chalk Farm Road, NW1
(020) 7722 0070

48 Battersea Rise, SW11
(020) 7924 2572

128 Westbourne Park Road, W2
(020) 7229 77770

8–10 Grove Vale, SE22
(020) 7737 7171

SAFETY

Police
Agar Street, Charing Cross, WC2
(020) 7730 1212

Accident and emergency
University College Hospital, 235 Euston Road, WC1
0845 155 5000

Doctor
The London Clinic, 20 Devonshire Place, W1
(020) 7935 4444

NHS dentist
Eastman Dental Hospital, 256 Gray's Inn Road, WC1
(020) 7915 1000

Pharmacy
Boots, 285 Oxford Street, WC1
(020) 7629 2105

Family planning
Chesterfield Clinic, 129 Harley Street, N1
(020) 7935 6776

Rape helpline
Haven Paddington
(020) 7886 1101

Fire and rescue service
London Fire Brigade, 8 Albert Embankment, SE1
(020) 7587 2000

Tube Tips

Itchy Tube Tips

All the gubbins you could possibly need on where to find your hangover brekkie, a power lunch, a hearty dinner or a late drink, whichever tube stop you wind up stumbling out of. We've got Zone 1 and 2 covered, with a few out of town extras thrown in for good measure (come on, we've all fallen asleep on the night bus with our faces in a bag of chips at some stage). If you've just discovered an absolute gem on your doorstep, drop us a line: editor@itchymedia.co.uk and we'll bob it in the books next year. So, travelcards at the ready...

🚇 ALDGATE
BREAKFAST **Judy's**
86 Whitechapel High St,
(020) 7375 1636
LUNCH **Barcelona Tapas**
15 St Botolph St,
(020) 7377 5111
DINNER **New Tayyabs**
83 Fieldgate St,
(020) 7247 9543
DRINK **The Golden Heart**
110 Commercial St,
(020) 7247 2158

🚇 ALDGATE EAST
BREAKFAST **Beigel Bake**
55 Charterhouse St,
(020) 7729 0616
LUNCH **Little Bay**
76 Commercial St,
(020) 7247 6097
DINNER **Sweet & Spicy**
40 Brick Ln,
(020) 7247 1081
DRINK **Vibe Bar**
91-95 Brick Ln,
(020) 7377 2899

🚇 ANGEL
BREAKFAST **Alpino**
97 Chapel Mkt,
(020) 7837 8330
LUNCH **Tartuf**
88 Upper St,
(020) 7288 0954
DINNER **Afghan Kitchen**
35 Islington Grn,
(020) 7359 8019
DRINK **Kings Head**
115 Upper St,
(020) 7226 0364

🚇 ARCHWAY
BREAKFAST **Toll Gate**
6 Archway Cl,
(020) 7687 2066
LUNCH **Nid Ting**
533 Holloway Rd,
(020) 7263 0506
DINNER **Sitara**
784 Holloway Rd,
(020) 7281 0649
DRINK **Settle Inn**
17-19 Archway Rd,
(020) 7272 7872

🚇 ARSENAL
BREAKFAST **Judy's**
249 Holloway Rd,
No phone
LUNCH **Golden Fish Bar**
98 Gillespie Rd,
(020) 7359 8364
DINNER **Iznik**
19 Highbury Pk,
(020) 7354 5697
DRINK **Highbury Barn**
26 Highbury Pk ,
(020) 7226 2383

🚇 BAKER ST
BREAKFAST **Café Arizona**
134 Marylebone St,
(020) 7935 0858
LUNCH **Fabrizio**
10 Paddington St,
(020) 7224 2556
DINNER **The Providores**
109 Marylebone High St,
(020) 7935 6175
DRINK **Prince Regent**
71 Marylebone High St,
(020) 7467 3811

🚇 BANK
BREAKFAST **Corney & Barrow**
2b East Chp ,
(020) 7929 3220
LUNCH **Browns**
8 Old Jewry,
(020) 7606 6677
DINNER **1 Lombard St**
1 Lombard St,
(020) 7929 6611
DRINK **City Tup**
66 Gresham St,
(020) 7606 8176

🚇 BARBICAN
BREAKFAST **Smiths**
67-77 Charterhouse St,
(020) 7251 7950
LUNCH **Cicada**
171 Farringdon Rd,
(020) 7608 1550
DINNER **Moro**
34-36 Exmouth Mkt,
(020) 7833 8336
DRINK **Charterhouse**
38 Charterhouse St,
(020) 7608 0858

🚇 BARON'S CT
BREAKFAST **Bonjour Tamar**
111 Hammersmith Rd,
(020) 7603 6334
LUNCH **Harvest Brasserie**
149 North End Rd,
(020) 1602 2591
DINNER **Cotto**
44 Blythe Rd,
(020) 7602 9333
DRINK **Queen's Head**
13 Brook Gm,
(020) 7603 3174

🚇 BAYSWATER
BREAKFAST **Café Fresco**
25 Westbourne Gro,
(020) 7221 2355
LUNCH **Khan's**
13-15 Westbourne Gro,
(020) 7727 5420
DINNER **Royal China**
13 Queensway,
(020) 7221 2535
DRINK **Rat & Parrot**
99 Queensway,
(020) 7727 0259

🚇 BELSIZE PK
BREAKFAST **Chamomile**
45 England's Ln,
(020) 7586 4580
LUNCH **Giacobazzi's Deli**
150 Fleet St,
(020) 7267 7222
DINNER **Weng Wah House**
240 Haverstock Hl,
(020) 7431 8620
DRINK **White Horse**
154 Fleet Rd,
(020) 7485 2112

🚇 BERMONDSEY
BREAKFAST **Food Junkie**
168 Jamaica Rd,
(020) 7237 9416
LUNCH **The Garrison**
99-101 Bermondsey St,
(020) 7089 9355
DINNER **Arancia**
52 Southwark Pk Rd,
(020) 7394 1751
DRINK **The Angel**
101 Bermondsey Wall,
(020) 7237 3608

🚇 BETHNAL GREEN

BREAKFAST Pellicci's
332 Bethnal Green Rd,
(020) 7739 4873
LUNCH Noodle King
185 Bethnal Green Rd,
(020) 7613 3131
DINNER The Fish Plaice
86 Cambridge Heath Rd,
(020) 7790 3254
DRINK Approach Tavern
47 Approach Rd,
(020) 8980 2321

🚇 BLACKFRIARS

BREAKFAST Bon Appetit IV
181 Queen Victoria St,
(020) 7236 0305
LUNCH Stamfords
7-8 Milroy Wlk,
(020) 7633 0256
DINNER Oxo Tower
Barge House St,
(020) 7803 3888
DRINK Cheshire Cheese
145 Fleet St,
(020) 7353 6170

🚇 BOND ST

BREAKFAST Appennino
38 James St,
(020) 7935 3970
LUNCH Chada Chada
16-17 Picton Pl,
(020) 7935 8212
DINNER Iguazu
Selfridges,
(020) 7318 3937
DRINK Lamb & Flag
24 James St,
(020) 7408 0132

🚇 BOROUGH

BREAKFAST Riva
Borough High St,
(020) 7407 0737
LUNCH Tas
33 The Cut,
(020) 7928 1444
DINNER Tower Tandoori
74-76 Tower Bridge Rd,
(020) 7237 3126
DRINK The Dover
6a Great Dover St,
(020) 7403 7773

🚇 BOW RD

BREAKFAST Orange Rooms
63 Burdett Rd,
(020) 8980 7336
LUNCH The Crown
223 Grove Rd,
(020) 8981 9998
DINNER Venus in the Park
552 Mile End Rd,
(020) 8880 6634
DRINK Lord Tredegar
50 Lichfield Rd,
(020)

🚇 BRIXTON

BREAKFAST SW9
11 Dorrell Pl,
(020) 7738 3116
LUNCH Bamboula
12 Acre Ln,
(020) 7737 6633
DINNER Satay Bar
447-455 Coldharbour Ln,
(020) 7326 5001
DRINK Living
443 Coldharbour Ln,
(020) 7326 4040

🚇 CALEDONIAN RD

BREAKFAST Parma Café
153 York Way,
(020) 7485 7609
LUNCH King's Pizza
280 Caledonian Rd,
(020) 7607 3434
DINNER Hemingford Arms
158 Hemingford Rd,
(020) 7607 3303
DRINK Shillibeer's
Carpenters Ms,
(020) 7700 1858

🚇 CAMDEN TOWN

BREAKFAST Bar Gansa
2 Inverness St,
(020) 7267 8909
LUNCH Wagamama
11 Jamestown Rd,
(020) 7428 0800
DINNER The Lock Tavern
35 Chalk Farm Rd,
(020) 7482 7163
DRINK WKD
18 Kentish Town Rd,
(020) 7267 1869

🚇 CANADA WATER

BREAKFAST Food Junkie
168 Jamaica Rd,
(020) 7237 9416
LUNCH GB Kebabs
153 Lower Rd,
(020) 7237 8064
DINNER Il Bordello
81 Wapping St,
(020) 7481 9950
DRINK Spice Island
163 Rotherhithe St,
(020) 7394 7108

🚇 CANARY WHARF

BREAKFAST Fresco Café
15 Cabot Sq,
(020) 7512 9072
LUNCH Singapore Sam
Cabot Pl West,
(020) 7513 2754
DINNER Carluccio's
2 Nash Ct,
(020) 7719 1749
DRINK The Grape
76 Narrow St,
(020) 7987 4396

🚇 CANNON ST

BREAKFAST Insalata
122 Cannon St,
(020) 7283 7776
LUNCH Sweetings
39 Queen Victoria St,
(020) 7248 3062
DINNER Fifteen 05
All Hallows Ln,
(020) 7283 1505
DRINK The Cannon
95 Cannon St,
(020) 7397 9881

🚇 CHALK FARM

BREAKFAST Le Tea Cosy
51A Regent's Pk,
(020) 7483 3378
LUNCH Marine Ices
8 Haverstock Hl,
(020) 7482 9003
DINNER Lemonia
89 Regent's Park Rd,
(020) 7586 7454
DRINK Queens
49 Regent's Park Rd,
(020) 7586 0408

🚇 CHANCERY LANE

BREAKFAST Tiffin's
24 Leather Ln,
(020) 7404 5894
LUNCH Traditional Plaice
83 Leather Ln,
(020) 7405 8277
DINNER Aki Japanese Bistro
182 Gray's Inn Rd,
(020) 7837 9019
DRINK Ye Olde Mitre
1 Ely Ct,
(020) 7405 4751

🚇 CHARING CROSS

BREAKFAST Ha! Ha! Bar
6 Villers St,
(020) 7930 1263
LUNCH Thai Square
148 The Strand,
020 7497 0904
DINNER Biagio Trattoria
17 Villiers St,
(020) 7839 3633
DRINK Gordon's
47 Villier's St,
(020) 7930 1408

🚇 CLAPHAM COMM.

BREAKFAST Gastro
67 Venn St,
(020) 7627 0222
LUNCH Pepper Tree
19 Clapham Common,
(020) 7622 1758
DINNER Kasbah
73 Venn St,
(020) 7498 3622
DRINK SO:UK
165 Clapham High St,
(020) 7622 4004

🚇 CLAPHAM NORTH

BREAKFAST Mario's Café
122 Clapham St,
(020)
LUNCH Alba
3 Bedford Rd,
(020) 7733 3636
DINNER La Gruta Café
91 Landor Rd,
(020) 7738 7392
DRINK Arch 635
15-16 Lendel Terrace,
(020) 7720 7343

Tube Tips

CLAPHAM SOUTH

BREAKFAST **Fuel**
27 Balham Hl,
(020) 8675 5333
LUNCH **Pizza On the Green**
4 Cavendish Pde,
(020) 8673 3227
DINNER **Bombay Bicycle**
95 Nightingale Ln,
(020) 8673 6217
DRINK **Firefly**
69 Clapham Common Sth,
(020) 8673 9162

COVENT GARDEN

BREAKFAST **Frank's Café**
52 Neal St,
(020) 7863 6345
LUNCH **Food For Thought**
31 Neal St,
(020) 7863 9072
DINNER **Boulevard Brasserie**
38-40 Wellington St,
(020) 7240 2992
DRINK **Fuel**
21 The Mkt ,
(020) 7836 2137

EARL'S CT

BREAKFAST **Troubadour**
265 Old Brompton Rd,
(020) 7370 1434
LUNCH **Krungtap**
227 Old Brompton Rd,
(020) 7259 2314
DINNER **The Little French**
18 Hogarth Pl,
(020) 7370 0366
DRINK **Balans West**
249 Old Brompton Rd,
(020) 7244 8838

EAST PUTNEY

BREAKFAST **Café Rogerio's**
157 High St,
(020) 8780 1988
LUNCH **La Mancha**
32 Putney High St,
(020) 8780 1022
DINNER **Ghillies**
894 Point Pleasant,
(020) 8871 9267
DRINK **Coat & Badge**
8 Lacy Rd,
(020) 8788 4900

EDGWARE RD

BREAKFAST **Millennium**
10 Bouverie Pl,
(020) 7706 4065
LUNCH **Barista Coffee**
5 Edgware Rd,
(020) 8952 4004
DINNER **Patogh**
8 Crawford Pl,
(020) 7262 4015
DRINK **Royal Exchange**
26 Sale Pl,
(020) 7723 3781

ELEPHANT&CASTLE

BREAKFAST **Court Café**
38 Newington Cswy,
(020) 7378 0176
LUNCH **The Lobster Pot**
3 Kenington Ln,
(020) 7582 5556
DINNER **Pizzeria Castello**
20 Walworth St,
(020) 7703 2556
DRINK **Ministry of Sound**
103 Gaunt St,
(020) 7378 6528

EMBANKMENT

BREAKFAST **Ha! Ha! Bar**
6 Villers St,
(020) 7930 1263
LUNCH **Hispaniola**
Victoria Emb,
(020) 7839 3011
DINNER **Biagio Trattoria**
17 Villers St,
(020) 7839 3633
DRINK **Queen Mary**
Victoria Emb,
(020) 7240 9404

EUSTON

BREAKFAST **Sorrento**
8 Woburn Wlk,
(020) 7388 3554
LUNCH **TaZu**
37 Chalton St,
(020) 7388 0808
DINNER **Chutneys**
124 Drummond St,
(020) 7388 0604
DRINK **Royal George**
8-14 Eversholt St,
(020) 7387 2431

EUSTON SQ

BREAKFAST **Rive Gauche**
20-21 Warren St,
(020) 7387 8232
LUNCH **Great Nepalese**
48 Eversholt St,
(020) 7388 6737
DINNER **Raavi Kebab**
125 Drummond St,
(020) 7388 1780
DRINK **Positively 4th Street**
119 Hampstead Rd,
(020) 7388 5380

FARRINGDON

BREAKFAST **Al's Bar Café**
11-13 Exmouth Mkt,
(020) 7837 4821
LUNCH **Little Bay**
171 Farringdon Road,
(020) 7278 1234
DINNER **Fluid**
40 Charterhouse St,
(020) 7253 3444
DRINK **Charterhouse**
38 Charterhouse St,
(020) 7608 0858

FINCHLEY RD

BREAKFAST **Joe's Patisserie**
3 Goldhurst Terrace,
(020) 7328 2295
LUNCH **Just around...**
446 Finchley Rd,
(020) 7431 3300
DINNER **Green Cottage**
9 New College Pde,
(020) 7722 5305
DRINK **Duke of Hamilton**
23-25 New End,
(020) 7794 0258

FINSBURY PK

BREAKFAST **Banners**
21 Park Rd,
(020) 8348 2930
LUNCH **La Porchetta**
147 Stroud Green Rd,
(020) 7281 2892
DINNER **Hummingbird**
84 Stroud Green Rd,
(020) 7263 9690
DRINK **Faltering Fullback**
19 Perth Rd,
(020) 7272 5834

FULHAM BDWY

BREAKFAST **Vingt Quatre**
325 Fulham Rd,
(020) 7376 7224
LUNCH **1492**
404 North End Rd,
(020) 7381 3810
DINNER **Wine & Kebab**
343 Fulham Rd,
(020) 7352 0967
DRINK **Black Bull**
358 Fulham Rd,
(020) 7376 7370

GLOUCESTER RD

BREAKFAST **La Liaison**
130 Gloucester Rd,
(020) 7370 3189
LUNCH **Jakobs**
20 Gloucester Rd,
(020) 7581 9292
DINNER **Bombay Brasserie**
Courtfield Rd,
(020) 7370 4040
DRINK **Drayton Arms**
153 Old Brompton Rd,
(020) 7835 2301

GOLDHAWK RD

BREAKFAST **Adam's Café**
111 Shepherds Bush Rd,
(020) 7602 2798
LUNCH **Sodere**
143 Goldhawk Road ,
(020) 8811 8011
DINNER **Bush Bar & Grill**
45a Goldhawk Rd,
(020) 8746 2111
DRINK **Vesbar**
15-19 Goldhawk Rd,
(020) 8762 0215

GOODGE ST

BREAKFAST **Italiano**
46 Goodge St,
(020) 7580 9688
LUNCH **Pizza Paradiso**
35 Store St,
(020) 7255 2554
DINNER **Pescatori**
57 Charlotte St,
(020) 7580 3289
DRINK **Fitzroy Tavern**
16 Charlotte St,
(020) 7580 3714

⊖ GT PORTLAND ST

BREAKFAST Villandry
170 Great Portland St,
(020) 7631 3131
LUNCH The Four Lanterns
96 Cleveland St,
(020) 7387 0704
DINNER Istanbul Meze
100 Cleveland St,
(020) 7387 0785
DRINK Market Place
11 Market Pl,
(020) 7079 2020

⊖ GREEN PK

BREAKFAST Mona Lisa
19 Landsdowne Row,
(020) 7253 1612
LUNCH The Ritz
Piccadilly,
(020) 7493 8181
DINNER Chez Gerard
31 Dover St,
(020) 7499 8171
DRINK Zeta
35 Hertford St,
(020) 7208 4067

⊖ HAMMERSMITH

BREAKFAST Maison Moulin
12 Hammersmith Brdwy,
(020) 8748 4438
LUNCH The George
28 Hammersmith Brdwy,
(020) 8748 9474
DINNER The Garden
1 Shortlands ,
(020) 8741 1555
DRINK The Dove
19 Upper Mall,
(020) 8748 5405

⊖ HAMPSTEAD

BREAKFAST Bagel Street
Oriel Pl,
(020) 7431 6709
LUNCH DimT Café
3 Heath St,
(020) 7435 0024
DINNER Bacchus Taverna
37 Heath St,
(020) 7435 1855
DRINK Spaniard's Inn
Spaniard's Road,
(020) 8731 6571

⊖ HIGH ST KEN

BREAKFAST Balans
187 Kensington High St,
(020) 7376 0115
LUNCH Papaya Tree
209 Kensington High St,
(020) 7937 2260
DINNER Cuba
11-13 Kensington High St,
(020) 7937 4137
DRINK Jimmy's
18 Kensington Church St,
(020) 7937 9988

⊖ HIGHBURY&IS

BREAKFAST Gill Wing
300 St Paul's Rd,
(020) 7226 2885
LUNCH La Piragua
176 Upper St,
(020) 7354 2843
DINNER Gem
265 Upper St,
(020) 7359 0405
DRINK Medicine Bar
181 Upper St,
(020) 7704 9536

⊖ HOLBORN

BREAKFAST Don Quixote
101 Kingsway,
(020) 7430 2413
LUNCH Fryer's Delight
19 Theobold's Rd ,
(020) 7405 4114
DINNER Edokko
50 Red Lion St,
(020) 7242 3490
DRINK Sway
61-65 Great Queen St,
(020) 7404 6114

⊖ HOLLAND PK

BREAKFAST Tootsies
120 Holland Park Av,
(020) 7229 8567
LUNCH The Aix
81 Holland Pk,
(020) 7727 7288
DINNER Royal Tandoori
184 Holland Park Av,
(020) 7603 4778
DRINK Prince of Wales
14 Princedale Rd,
(020) 7313 9321

⊖ HOLLOWAY RD

BREAKFAST Café L'Arome
256 Holloway Rd,
(020) 7607 5965
LUNCH Iznik
19 Highbury Pk,
(020) 7354 5697
DINNER El Molino
379 Holloway Rd,
(020) 7700 4312
DRINK Spoofer's Bar
North London University,
(020) 7607 2622

⊖ HYDE PK CORNER

BREAKFAST Knightsbridge
5-6 William St,
(020) 7235 4040
LUNCH Pizza on the Park
171 Farringdon Rd,
(020) 7278 1234
DINNER Salloos
62-64 Kinnerton St,
(020) 7235 4444
DRINK Mandarin Bar
66 Knightsbridge,
(020) 7235 2000

⊖ KENNINGTON

BREAKFAST Kennington Lane
205-209 Kennington Ln,
(020) 7793 8313
LUNCH The Painted Heron
205-209 Kennington Ln,
(020) 7793 8313
DINNER Dog House
293 Kennington Rd,
(020) 7820 9310
DRINK La Finca
185 Kennington Lane ,
(020) 7735 1061

⊖ KENSAL GRN

BREAKFAST Nest-Café
549 Harrow Rd,
(020) 8964 3953
LUNCH Manhattan Pizza
20 Station Ter,
(020) 89660 4179
DINNER Paradise
19 Kilburn Ln,
(020) 8969 0098
DRINK William IV
786 Harrow Rd,
(020) 8969 5944

⊖ KENSINGTON

BREAKFAST Frank's
3 Station Arcade,
(020) 8741 4839
LUNCH Bonjour Tamarr
113 Hammersmith Rd,
(020) 7603 6334
DINNER Apadana
351 Kensington High St,
(020) 7603 3696
DRINK The Queen's Head
13 Brook Grn,
(020) 7603 3174

⊖ KENTISH TOWN

BREAKFAST Mario's Café
6 Kelly St,
(020) 7284 2066
LUNCH Bengal Lancer
253 Kentish Town Rd,
(020) 7485 6688
DINNER Café Renoir
244 Kentish Town Rd,
(020) 7485 7186
DRINK Peachykeen
112 Kentish Town Rd,
(020) 7482 2300

⊖ KILBURN

BREAKFAST Cookies & Cream
321-323 Kilburn High Rd,
(020) 7328 9262
LUNCH No 77
77 Mill Ln,
(020) 7435 7787
DINNER Small & Beautiful
351-353 Kilburn High Rd,
(020) 7328 2637
DRINK Brondes Age
328 Kilburn High Rd,
(020) 7604 3887

⊖ KILBURN PK

BREAKFAST Little Bay
228 Belsize Rd,
(020) 7372 4699
LUNCH Tasty Kebabs
39 Kilburn High Rd,
(020) 7624 8414
DINNER Beirut Cellar
248 Belsize Rd,
(020) 7328 3472
DRINK The Bird in Hand
12 West End Ln,
(020) 7328 1477

Tube Tips

➜ KING'S CROSS

BREAKFAST **Café Plaka**
315 Gray's Inn Rd,
(020) 7833 5823
LUNCH **Canal 125**
125 Caledonian Rd,
(020) 7837 1924
DINNER **Islington Hilton**
53 Upper St,
(020) 7354 7700
DRINK **Water Rats**
328 Gray's Inn Rd,
(020) 7837 7269

➜ KNIGHTSBRIDGE

BREAKFAST **Knightsbridge**
5-6 William St,
(020) 7235 4040
LUNCH **Wagamama**
109-125 Knightsbridge,
(020) 7235 5000
DINNER **Borshtch 'n' Tears**
45 Beauchamp Pl,
(020) 7589 5003
DRINK **Mandarin Bar**
66 Knightsbridge,
(020) 7235 2000

➜ LADBROKE GROVE

BREAKFAST **Uncle's**
305 Portobello Rd,
(020) 8962 0090
LUNCH **The Grain Shop**
269a Portobello Rd,
(020) 7279 5571
DINNER **Osteria Basilico**
29 Kensington Park Rd,
(020) 7324 4455t
DRINK **The Pelican** 140-
45 All Saints' Rd,
(020) 7792 3073

➜ LAMBETH NORTH

BREAKFAST **Perdoni's**
18-20 Kennington High Rd,
(020) 7253 1612
LUNCH **The Fire Station**
150 Waterloo Rd,
(020) 7620 2226
DINNER **Cubana**
48 Lower Marsh,
(020) 7928 8778
DRINK **BRB at The Tankard**
111 Kennington Rd,
(020) 7820 3682

➜ LATIMER RD

BREAKFAST **Embassy Café**
1 Mortimer Sq,
(020) 7243 1676
LUNCH **Notting Grill**
123A Clarendon Rd,
(020) 7229 1500
DINNER **The Station**
41 Bramley Rd,
(020) 7229 1111
DRINK **Kenilworth Castle**
104 St Ann's Rd,
(020) 7727 0656

➜ LEICESTER SQ

BREAKFAST **Stockpot**
38 Panton St,
(020) 7839 5142
LUNCH **New World**
1 Gerrard Pl,
(020) 7734 0396
DINNER **Bar Italia**
22 Frith St,
(020) 7437 4520
DRINK **Zoo Bar**
13-18 Bear St,
(020) 7839 4188

➜ LIVERPOOL ST

BREAKFAST **Mr Frothy**
Brushfield Street,
(020)
LUNCH **The Light**
233 Shoreditch High St,
(020) 7247 8989
DINNER **Tatsuso**
32 Broadgate Circle,
(020) 7638 5863
DRINK **Herbal**
12/14 Kingsland Rd,
(020) 7613 4462

➜ LONDON BRIDGE

BREAKFAST **Borough Café**
11 Park St,
(020) 7407 5048
LUNCH **Anchor Bankside**
34 Park St,
(020) 7407 1577
DINNER **Georgetown**
London Bridge St,
(020) 7357 7359
DRINK **Wicked**
4 Tooley St,
(020) 7403 6777

➜ MAIDA VALE

BREAKFAST **Raoul's Express**
10 Clifton Rd,
(020) 7289 6649
LUNCH **Blah Blah Blah**
28 Clifton Rd,
(020) 7289 6399
DINNER **Biblos**
1-3 Sutherland Av,
(020) 7432 8782
DRINK **The Warrington**
93 Warrington Crs,
(020) 7253 7234

➜ MANSION HOUSE

BREAKFAST **Chapters Deli**
70 Cannon St,
(020) 7248 3034
LUNCH **Fifteen 05**
All Hallows Ln,
(020) 7283 1505
DINNER **Silks & Spice**
11 Queen Victoria St,
(020) 7248 7878
DRINK **Ye Olde Watling**
29 Watling St,
(020) 7653 9971

➜ MARBLE ARCH

BREAKFAST **Mosco's Café**
26 North Audley St,
(020) 7493 0090
LUNCH **The Terrace**
30 Portman Sq,
(020) 7486 5800
DINNER **Maroush**
21 Edgware Rd,
(020) 7723 0773
DRINK **Mason's Arms**
51 Berkeley St,
(020) 7723 2131

➜ MARYLEBONE

BREAKFAST **Raw Deal**
65 York St,
(020) 7262 4841
LUNCH **Garbo**
42 Crawford St,
(020) 7262 6582
DINNER **Sea Shell**
49-51 Lisson Gv,
(020) 7224 9000
DRINK **Feathers**
43 Linhope St,
(020) 7402 1327

➜ MILE END

BREAKFAST **Orange Rooms**
63 Burdett Rd,
(020) 8980 7336
LUNCH **Matsu**
558 Mile End Rd,
(020) 8983 3528
DINNER **Britannia Fish Bar**
101 Grove Rd,
(020) 8983 3414
DRINK **Royal Inn**
111 Lauriston Rd,
(020) 8985 3321

➜ MONUMENT

BREAKFAST **Corney & Barrow**
2b Eastcheap,
(020) 7929 3220
LUNCH **TK's**
31 Lovat Ln,
(020) 7220 7613
DINNER **Prism**
147 Leadenhall St,
(020) 7256 3888
DRINK **City Tup**
66 Gersham St,
(020) 7606 8176

➜ MOORGATE

BREAKFAST **Smiths**
67-77 Charterhouse St,
(020) 7251 7950
LUNCH **Nylon**
11 Addle St,
(020) 7600 7771
DINNER **Sushi & Soza**
Moorgate Station,
(020) 7638 3866
DRINK **The Globe**
Moorgate,
(020) 7786 9241

➜ MORN. CRES.

BREAKFAST **Sandwich, etc**
269 Eversholt St,
(020) 7387 6402
LUNCH **El Parador**
245 Eversholt St,
(020) 7387 2789
DINNER **Asakusa**
265 Eversholt St,
(020) 7388 8533
DRINK **The Crown**
100 Arlington Rd,
(020) 7485 8008

← NEW CROSS

BREAKFAST **New Cross Café**
365 New Cross Rd,
(020) 8692 3544
LUNCH **A J Goddard**
203 Deptford High St,
(020) 8692 3601
DINNER **Alanya**
164 New Cross Rd,
(020) 7639 3751
DRINK **Goldsmith's Tavern**
316 New Cross Rd,
(020) 8692 3193

← N. GREENWICH

BREAKFAST **Holiday Inn**
Bugsby Way,
(087) 0400 9670
LUNCH **Memsaheb**
65-67 Amsterdam Rd,
(020) 7538 3008
DINNER **The Gun**
27 Cold Harbour,
(020) 7515 5222
DRINK **Pilot Inn**
68 River Way,
(020) 8858 5910

← NOTTING HILL

BREAKFAST **Dakota**
127 Ledbury Rd,
(020) 7792 9191
LUNCH **New Culture**
157-159 Notting Hill Gate,
(020) 7313 9688
DINNER **Café Mandola**
139-141 Westbourne Grv,
(020) 7229 4734
DRINK **The Gate**
87 Notting Hill Gate,
(020) 7727 9007

← OLD ST

BREAKFAST **Cantaloupe**
35 Charlotte Rd,
(020) 7613 4411
LUNCH **La Scala**
74 Luke St,
(020) 7613 1230
DINNER **Yelo**
8-9 Hoxton Sq,
(020) 7729 4626
DRINK **Mother**
Above 333 Old St,
(020) 7739 5949

← OVAL

BREAKFAST **Oval Café**
312 Kennington Park Rd
(020) 7735 4603
LUNCH **The Timegad**
5 Brixton Station Rd,
(020) 7737 1809
DINNER **Lavender**
171 Lavender Hill,
(020) 7978 5242
DRINK **The Fentiman Arms**
64 Fentiman Rd,
(020) 7793 9796

← OXFORD CIRCUS

BREAKFAST **Bar Chocolate**
27 D'Arblay St,
(020) 7287 2923
LUNCH **Léon**
35-36 Gt Marlborough St
(020) 7437 5280
DINNER **Kerala**
15 Great Castle St,
(020) 7580 2125
DRINK **Mash**
19-21 Great Portland St,
(020) 7637 5555

← PADDINGTON

BREAKFAST **Caffé Nero**
Paddington Station,
(020) 7402 0417
LUNCH **Indus Delta**
135 Praed St,
(020) 7723 3191
DINNER **Los Remos**
38 Southwick St,
(020) 7706 1870
DRINK **Steam**
1 Eastbourne Ter,
(020) 7850 0555

← PARSON'S GRN

BREAKFAST **Tootsies**
177 New Kings Rd,
(020) 7736 4023
LUNCH **The Durrell**
704 Fulham Rd,
(020) 7736 3014
DINNER **Pappa & Ciccia**
105 Munster Rd,
(020) 7384 1884
DRINK **Havana**
490 Fulham Rd,
(020) 7381 5005

← PICCADILLY CIRCUS

BREAKFAST **The Stockpot**
38 Panton St,
(020) 7839 5142
LUNCH **Le Pigalle**
11 Berwick St,
(020) 7734 5144
DINNER **Misato**
11 Wardour St,
(020) 7734 0808
DRINK **The Astor**
20 Glasshouse St,
(020) 7734 4888

← PIMLICO

BREAKFAST **Relish**
8 John Islip St,
(020) 7828 0628
LUNCH **Grumbles**
35 Churlton St,
(020) 7834 0149
DINNER **Top Curry**
3 Lupus St,
0871 332 0242
DRINK **Elusive Camel**
27 Gillingham St,
(020) 7233 9004

← PUTNEY

BREAKFAST **The Garden Café**
93 Charlwood St,
(020) 7821 7576
LUNCH **Kazbar**
24 Putney High St,
(020) 8780 0929
DINNER **La Mancha**
32 Putney High St,
(020) 8780 1022
DRINK **Coast**
50-54 High St,
(020) 8780 8931

← QUEEN'S PK

BREAKFAST **Hugo's**
25 Lonsdale Rd,
(020) 7372 1232
LUNCH **The Sundarban**
77 Salusbury Road ,
(020) 7624 8852
DINNER **Penk's**
79 Salusbury Road,
(020) 7736 2115
DRINK **The Greyhound**
50-52 Salusbury Road,
(020) 7328 3286

← QUEENSWAY

BREAKFAST **Café Fresco**
25 Westbourne Grv,
(020) 7221 2355
LUNCH **Khan's**
13-15 Westbourne Grv,
(020) 7727 5420
DINNER **Royal China**
13 Queensway,
(020) 7221 2535
DRINK **The King's Head**
33 Moscow Rd,
(020) 7229 4233

← RAYNERS LANE

BREAKFAST **Imperial Café**
236 Imperial Dr,
(020) 8868 1189
LUNCH **Papaya**
15 Village Way East,
(020) 8866 5582
DINNER **Silver Dollar**
230 Imperial Dr,
(020) 8866 9226
DRINK **The Village Inn**
402–408 Rayners Ln,
(020) 8868 8551

← REGENT'S PK

BREAKFAST **Villandry**
170 Great Portland St,
(020) 7631 3131
LUNCH **Queen's Head**
30–32 Albany St,
(020) 7916 6206
DINNER **Getti**
42 Marylebone High St,
020 7486 3753
DRINK **Dover Castle**
43 Weymouth Mews,
(020) 7580 4412

← ROTHERHITHE

BREAKFAST **Fish King**
11 Plough Way,
(020) 8980 1042
LUNCH **Fish King**
11 Plough Way,
(020) 8980 1042
DINNER **The Angel**
101 Bermondsey Wall,
(020) 7237 3608
DRINK **Spice Island**
163 Rotherhithe Street,
(020) 7394 7108

Tube Tips

ROYAL OAK

BREAKFAST **Café Bijou**
1 Sutherland Av,
(020) 7432 8782
LUNCH **The Westbourne**
101 Westbourne Park Vls,
(020) 7221 1332
DINNER **Anthony's**
54 Porcester Rd,
(020) 7243 8743
DRINK **Royal Oak**
88 Bishops Bridge Rd,
(020) 7229 2886

RUSSELL SQ

BREAKFAST **Café Romano**
11 Grenville St,
(020) 7278 6548
LUNCH **Duke of York**
7 Roger St,
(020) 7242 7230
DINNER **Wagamama**
40 Streatham St,
(020) 7323 9223
DRINK **AKA**
18 West Central St,
(020) 7836 0110

SOUTHWARK

BREAKFAST **Bankside Café**
142 Southwark St,
(020) 7928 2024
LUNCH **Baltic**
74 Blackfriars Rd,
(020) 7928 1111
DINNER **Bankside**
32 Southwark Bridge Rd,
(020) 7633 0011
DRINK **The Ring**
72 Blackfriars Rd,
(020) 7928 2589

ST JAMES'S PK

BREAKFAST **Broadway Café**
16 Broadway,
(020) 7222 2646
LUNCH **The Quilon**
41 Buckingham Gate,
(020) 7821 1899
DINNER **Inn the Park**
St James's Park,
(020) 7451 9999
DRINK **Two Chairmen**
39 Dartmouth St,
(020) 7222 8694

ST JOHN'S WOOD

BREAKFAST **Maison Blanc**
37 St John's Wood High St,
(020) 7586 1982
LUNCH **Caffe Uno**
122 St John's Wood High St,
(020) 7722 0400
DINNER **L'Aventure**
3 Blenheim Ter,
(020) 7624 6232
DRINK **The Salt House**
63 Abbey Rd,
(020) 7328 6626

ST PAUL'S

BREAKFAST **Café**
20 Little Britain,
(020) 5355 4489
LUNCH **The Refectory**
St Paul's Churchyard,
(020) 7246 8358
DINNER **Just The Bridge**
1 Paul's Walk,
(020) 7236 0000
DRINK **Balls Brothers**
6-8 Cheapside,
(020) 7248 2708

STAMFORD BRK

BREAKFAST **The Ritz**
340a King St,
(020) 8748 7517
LUNCH **Yellow River Café**
12 Chiswick High St,
(020) 8987 9791
DINNER **Anarkali**
303 King St,
(020) 8748 1760
DRINK **The Hart**
383 King St,
(020) 8748 6076

STEPNEY GRN

BREAKFAST **Funky Munky**
285 Whitechapel Rd,
(087) 1223 8192
LUNCH **Pride of Asia**
207 Mile End Rd,
(020) 7780 9321
DINNER **Taja**
199 Whitechapel Rd,
(020) 7247 3866
DRINK **New Globe**
359 Mile End Road,
(020) 8981 2800

STOCKWELL

BREAKFAST **Stockwell Café**
197 Stockwell Rd,
(020) 7274 1724
LUNCH **Rebato's**
169 South Lambeth Rd,
(020) 7735 6388
DINNER **Al Montanha**
71 Stockwell Rd,
(020) 7737 5961
DRINK **Circle Bar**
348 Clapham Rd,
(020) 7622 3683

SURREY QUAYS

BREAKFAST **Hubbub**
269 Westferry Rd,
(020) 7515 5577
LUNCH **G.B.Kebabs**
152 Lower Rd,
(020) 7237 8064
DINNER **The Angel**
101 Bermondsey Wall ,
(020) 7237 3608
DRINK **Spice Island**
163 Rotherhithe St,
(020) 7394 7108

SWISS COTTAGE

BREAKFAST **Café Arch**
17 Northways Pde,
(020) 7483 4089
LUNCH **Singapore Garden**
83 Fairfax Rd,
(020) 7328 5314
DINNER **Jimmy's Thai**
7 New College Pde,
(020) 7722 8474
DRINK **Elbow Room**
135 Finchley Rd,
(020) 7586 9888

TEMPLE

BREAKFAST **Pret a Manger**
421 The Strand,
(020) 7240 5900
LUNCH **Leith's**
113 Chancery Lane,
(020) 7278 1234
DINNER **The Admiralty**
150 The Strand,
(020) 7845 4646
DRINK **Edgar Wallace**
40 Essex St,
(020) 7343 3120

TOTT. CT RD

BREAKFAST **Bar Chocolate**
27 D'Arblay St,
(020) 7287 2823
LUNCH **Café Emm**
17 Frith St,
(020) 7437 0723
DINNER **Busaba Eathai**
106-110 Wardour St,
(020) 7255 8686
DRINK **Phoenix Artist Club**
1 Phoenix St,
(020) 7836 1077

TOWER HILL

BREAKFAST **Tower Patisserie**
St Katherine's Dock,
(020) 7481 1464
LUNCH **La Lanterna**
6 Mill St,
(020) 7252 3054
DINNER **Aquarium**
St Katherine's Dock,
(020) 7480 6116
DRINK **Dicken's Inn**
St Katherine's Dock,
(020) 7488 2208

TUFNELL PK

BREAKFAST **Dartmouth Arms**
35 York Rise,
(020) 7485 3267
LUNCH **Roma**
12 Dartmouth Park Hl,
(020) 7272 1164
DINNER **Lalibela**
137 Fortress Rd,
(020) 7284 0600
DRINK **Progress N7**
162 Tufnell Park Rd,
(020) 7272 2078

TURNHAM GRN

BREAKFAST **La Mirage**
309 Chiswick High Rd,
(020) 8994 1661
LUNCH **Dumela**
42 Devonshire Rd,
(020) 8742 3149
DINNER **West Kebab**
196 Chiswick High Rd,
(020) 8742 3617
DRINK **George IV**
185 Chiswick High Rd,
(020) 8994 4624

VAUXHALL

BREAKFAST **Pavilion Café**
New Covent Garden Mkt,
(020) 8466 7233
LUNCH **Bonnington Café**
11 Vauxhall Grv,
(020) 7820 7466
DINNER **Lavender**
112 Vauxhall Wlk,
(020) 7735 4440
DRINK **Royal Vauxhall**
372 Kennington Ln,
(020) 7582 0833

VICTORIA

BREAKFAST **Alpino**
8 Elizabeth St,
(020) 7730 8400
LUNCH **Christopher's**
Terminus Pl,
(020) 7976 5522
DINNER **Kazan**
93 Wilton Rd,
(020) 7233 7100
DRINK **The Speaker**
46 Great Peter St,
(020) 7222 1749

WAPPING

BREAKFAST **The Wall**
61 Wapping Wl,
(020) 7709 7887
LUNCH **Riverview Chinese**
16 New Crane Pl,
(020) 7480 6026
DINNER **Wapping Project**
Wapping Wl,
(020) 7608 2080
DRINK **Prospect of Whitby**
57 Wapping Wl,
(020) 7481 1095

WARREN ST

BREAKFAST **Rive Gauche**
20-21 Warren St,
(020) 7387 8232
LUNCH **Alicia**
23 Warren St,
(020) 7388 1414
DINNER **Anwars**
64 Grafton Way,
(020) 7387 6664
DRINK **Positively 4th Street**
119 Hampstead Rd,
(020) 7388 5380

WATERLOO

BREAKFAST **Etsu**
29 & 49 York Rd,
(020) 7620 1552
LUNCH **Masters Super Fish**
191 Waterloo Rd,
(020) 7928 6924
DINNER **Ned's Noodle Box**
3 Belvedere Rd,
(020) 7593 0077
DRINK **Anchor & Hope**
36 The Cut,
(020) 7928 9898

WARWICK AV

BREAKFAST **Lospuntino**
18, Formosa St,
(020) 7266 2043
LUNCH **Red Pepper**
8 Formosa St,
(020) 7266 2708
DINNER **Prince Alfred**
5a Formosa St,
(020) 7286 3287
DRINK **The Bridge House**
13 Westbourne Terrace Rd,
(087) 1984 1781

WEMBLEY PK

BREAKFAST **Moulin Grill**
139 Wembley Pk Dr,
(020) 8902 1799
LUNCH **The Ugly Duckling**
121 Wembley Pk Dr,
(020) 8900 1157
DINNER **New Kabana**
43 Blackbird Hl,
(020) 8200 7094
DRINK **The Torch**
1-5 Bridge Rd,
(020) 8904 5794

W. BROMPTON

BREAKFAST **Troubador**
265 Old Brompton Rd,
(020) 7370 1434
LUNCH **The Grill**
2-4 Lillie Rd,
(020) 7381 4339
DINNER **Atlas**
16 Seagrave Rd,
(020) 7385 9129
DRINK **Balans West**
239 Old Brompton Rd,
(020) 7244 8838

W. HAMPSTEAD

BREAKFAST **Mr Gingham**
112 West End Ln,
(020) 7253 1612
LUNCH **Yuzu**
102 Fortune Green Rd,
(020) 7431 6602
DINNER **The Gallery**
190 Broadhurst Gdns,
(020) 7625 9184
DRINK **Lately's**
175 West End Ln,
(020) 7625 6474

W. KENSINGTON

BREAKFAST **Continente**
62 North End Rd,
(020) 7603 6311
LUNCH **Millennium Café**
North End Road,
(020) 7278 1234
DINNER **Ta Krai**
100 North End Rd,
(020) 7386 5375
DRINK **Fox Rattle & Hum**
3 North End Crs,
(020) 7603 7006

WESTBOURNE PK

BREAKFAST **Mike's Café**
12 Blenheim Crs,
(020) 7229 3757
LUNCH **The Cedar**
65 Fernhead Rd,
(020) 8964 2011
DINNER **The Cow**
89 Westbourne Park Rd,
(020) 7221 0021
DRINK **Babushka**
41 Tavistock Crescent,
(020) 7727 9250

WESTMINSTER

BREAKFAST **Café Nero**
1-2 Bridge St,
(020) 7925 0781
LUNCH **The Footstool**
Smith Square,
(020) 7222 2779
DINNER **The Atrium**
4 Millbank,
(020) 7233 0032
DRINK **Red Lion**
48 Parliament St,
(020) 7930 5826

WHITE CITY

BREAKFAST **Sonia's Café**
308 Latimer Rd,
(020) 8746 8956
LUNCH **The Lunch Box**
235 Wood Ln,
(020) 8746 2365
DINNER **Fatima**
253 Wood Ln,
(020) 8749 1323
DRINK **Springbok**
51 South Africa,
(020) 8743 8476

WHITECHAPEL

BREAKFAST **Funky Munky**
285 Whitechapel Rd,
(020) 7377 5902
LUNCH **Nando's**
19 Mile End Rd
(020) 7729 5783
DINNER **Tayab Kebab**
9 Fieldgate St,
(020) 7247 9543
DRINK **Indo**
133 Whitechapel Rd,
(020) 7247 4826

WILLESDEN GRN

BREAKFAST **S & B**
351 Kilburn High Rd,
(020) 7328 2637
LUNCH **CoCo's Tapas**
41-43 High Rd,
(020) 8830 1638
DINNER **Shish**
2-6 Station Pde,
(020) 8208 9292
DRINK **Ned Kelly's**
305 High St,
(020) 8459 3020

WOOD GREEN

BREAKFAST **Villa Dei Fiori**
Shopping City Mkt Hall,
(020) 8365 8406
LUNCH **Vrisaki**
73 Myddleton Rd,
(020) 8889 8760
DINNER **Mosaica**
Clarendon Rd,
(020) 8889 2400
DRINK **The Nelson**
232-234 High Rd,
(087) 1984 4791

Index

Index

That's it for 2006, folks. We hope this guide has helped you squeeze every last drop of fun out of London Town. Thanks for letting us come along for the ride. We hope we'll see you again next year for more of the same shenanigans. That should give you plenty of time to work off the monster hangover. Lots of love, Team Itchy.